Britain and India
1845–1947

Tim Leadbeater

HODDER
EDUCATION
AN HACHETTE UK COMPANY

Study guides written by Angela Leonard (Edexcel).

The publishers would like to thank the following individuals, institutions and companies for permission to reproduce copyright illustrations in this book:
AKG-Images/Ullstein Bild, page 96 (bottom); © Austrian Archives/Corbis, page 63; © Bettmann/Corbis, pages 70, 87, 145; Henri Cartier-Bresson/Magnum Photos, page 128; © CORBIS, page 77; © Dinodia Images, pages 38, 110; Getty Images, pages 78, 83, 98, 111, 132; © Hulton-Deutsch Collection/Corbis, pages 32, 127; By permission of Llyfrgell Genedlaethol Cymru/National Library of Wales/Solo Syndication, pages 105, 119, 144; David Low, *The Daily News* and *The Star*, 16th December 1919/British Cartoon Archive, University of Kent/Solo Syndication, page 53; Paul Popper/Popperfoto/Getty Images, page 104; Private Collection, Archives Charmet/The Bridgeman Art Library, page 39; Private Collection, Ken Welsh/ The Bridgeman Art Library, pages 11, 13; Time & Life Pictures/Getty Images, pages 28, 84, 106.

The publishers would like to acknowledge use of the following extracts:
Basic Books for an extract from *Empire: The British Imperial Experience from 1765 to the Present* by Denis Judd, 1996; Basic Books for an extract from *Empire: The Rise and Demise of the British World Order* by Niall Ferguson, 2003; Cambridge University Press for an extract from *The Cambridge Illustrated History of the British Empire* by P.J. Marshall, 1996; Little Brown & Co. for an extract from *The Rise and Fall of the British Empire* by Lawrence James, 1994; Oxford University Press, USA for an extract from *Modern India: The Origins of an Asian Democracy* by Judith M. Brown, 1994; Penguin Books, India for extracts from *India's Struggle for Independence* by Bipan Chandra, 1988; Trafalgar Square Publishing for an extract from *Liberty or Death: India's Journey to Independence and Division* by Patrick French, 1997; Vikas Publishing House for extracts from *Towards India's Freedom and Partition* by S.R. Mehrotra, 1978.

Every effort has been made to trace and acknowledge ownership of copyright. The publishers will be glad to make suitable arrangements with any copyright holders whom it has not been possible to contact.

Hachette Livre UK's policy is to use papers that are natural, renewable and recyclable products and made from wood grown in sustainable forests. The logging and manufacturing processes are expected to conform to the environmental regulations of the country of origin.

Orders: please contact Bookpoint Ltd, 130 Milton Park, Abingdon, Oxon OX14 4SB. Telephone: (44) 01235 827720. Fax: (44) 01235 400454. Lines are open 9.00–5.00, Monday to Saturday, with a 24-hour message answering service. Visit our website at www.hoddereducation.co.uk

© Tim Leadbeater 2008
First published in 2008 by
Hodder Education,
An Hachette UK Company
338 Euston Road
London NW1 3BH

Impression number   5 4 3 2
Year   2012 2011 2010 2009

Cover photo shows a cartoon by Johnson in *Kladderadatsch*, 13 August 1933, 'Seated on the Indian elephant, whose tusks are blunted by the policy of non-violence, Gandhi defies the violence of the British Lion', courtesy of Mary Evans Picture Library
Typeset in Baskerville 10/12pt and produced by Gray Publishing, Tunbridge Wells
Printed in Malta

A catalogue record for this title is available from the British Library

ISBN: 978 0340 965 979

Contents

Dedication

Keith Randell (1943–2002)

The *Access to History* series was conceived and developed by Keith, who created a series to 'cater for students as they are, not as we might wish them to be'. He leaves a living legacy of a series that for over 20 years has provided a trusted, stimulating and well-loved accompaniment to post-16 study. Our aim with these new editions is to continue to offer students the best possible support for their studies.

Note

Historical anglicised names of cities and locations have been used in this book unless a specific modern reference is made. For example, Bombay is used rather than Mumbai but a modern international airport is at Kolkatta rather than Calcutta, the historical capital of British India.

1 The Subcontinent 1800–1900

POINTS TO CONSIDER

At the stroke of midnight between 14 and 15 August 1947, the nations of India and Pakistan came into existence. They gained or were granted, depending on the point of view, their independence from the British Empire. Three hundred million subjects of the King-Emperor George VI became citizens of modern democracies. The population of the Empire instantly shrank to one-fifth of its size. It was the largest peacetime transfer of power in history.

However, since then the two countries have gone to war with each other several times, usually over the disputed province of Kashmir, an unresolved problem of independence and partition. Both nations now possess nuclear weapons and the United Nations has identified the Kashmir conflict as the one most likely to escalate to nuclear war in the world today. In this context, the study of Indo-Pakistani independence could hardly be more important.

This chapter sets out the context of the nationalist movements for independence. The nineteenth-century period covers the most troubled and then the most confident time for the British Raj (rule). The British would not seize more territory after 1850 and treaties were negotiated with the Indian rulers of hundreds of independent states. In 1857–8, a mutiny or rebellion broke out which traumatised the British in India and Britain itself. In consequence, radical changes were made to the government of India. The system which was created would essentially stay the same until a few years before independence.

This chapter examines in more detail:

- The land and the people
- The Indian Mutiny
- The Raj and renaissance
- Imperialism and nationalism

Key dates
1600   Charter granted to East India Company by
        Elizabeth I
1857   Indian Mutiny began
1858   Crown control of India
        Royal Proclamation
1875   Foundation of Aligarh College
1877   Queen Victoria declared Empress, British
        territorial control in India at its greatest
1883   Ilbert Bill
1885   Formation of Congress Party
1892   Indian Councils Act
1919   Amritsar Massacre

1 | Introduction to the Land and People

The nationalist independence movement and the reactions of the British form a political and constitutional history. It is, however, important to understand something of the geographical, social, cultural and economic factors which underlie and shape this history. Partition took place as a result of religious pressures and along religious **demographic** lines and a basic understanding of this is crucial to what follows.

Geography

The subcontinent, sometimes referred to as South Asia, covers a landmass equivalent to Europe (excluding Russia) or about half the USA.

Three distinct geographical areas are customarily identified. By far the most significant is known as the Indo-Gangetic plain. This is an arc of extremely fertile, and swelteringly hot, territory running up the huge valley of the river Indus, now in Pakistan, across the area of the **Punjab** and down the equally huge valley of the river Ganges. The Ganges meets the river Brahmaputra flowing round from the north side of the Himalayas to form the largest delta system in the world in the area of Bengal, now Bangladesh. This region has been settled and farmed since prehistory and has been the territorial base of almost all the rulers of India. Both of the historical capitals of India, Delhi and Calcutta (modern Kolkata) lie within that arc.

To the north lie the Himalayas, the highest mountain range in the world and still rising as a result of the collision of tectonic plates. The political effect of this barrier, combined with the peninsular form of the subcontinent, has been that foreign invasions have come overwhelmingly from the Islamic north-west, the north-eastern approaches being even more difficult as a result of mountains, Burmese jungle and the Bengal delta swamp.

To the south of the plains, coastal strips provide opportunities for ports, cities and trade. Behind them rise the hills of the Western and Eastern Ghats creating inland the Deccan plateau.

Demographic
Relating to population.

Punjab
Meaning five rivers.

Key terms

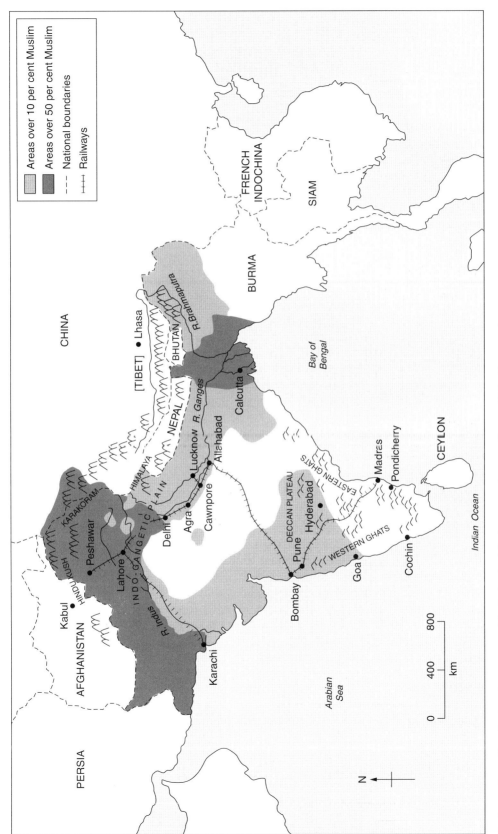

Indian subcontinent, showing geographical physical features, and proportions of Muslim people.

Ironically, this area has political significance because it is less fertile and populous. Invaders and rulers found it difficult or impossible to control. Civilisation and power flourished early and enduringly in the Indo-Gangetic plains but was necessarily more cosmopolitan and multicultural. The south, by contrast, was resistance territory and, in that sense, the Indian heartland.

Ethnic, religious and linguistic groups

Variation in the Indian population corresponds broadly to this geopolitical sketch but it must be recognised that there is a vast range of ethnic, religious and linguistic difference even for such a large area.

Hinduism is the core religion of India but in certain areas Islam, Sikhism and Buddhism are more prevalent. These will be treated under historical developments further below.

The peoples of the south speak languages of the Dravidian family, and Buddhism is a major religion. They are generally darker-skinned (and there remains some skin-colour prejudice against them within India). Some ethnic groups, notably the Tamils, are fighting for further independence. There is also still widespread resistance to the use of Hindi as a national language.

The peoples of the north speak languages of the Indo-European family which also embraces English, Scandinavian and Mediterranean languages. These peoples are lighter-skinned as a result of waves of central Asian (Aryan) incomers. Islam is a major religion and predominant in certain places.

In the Himalayan provinces, west and east, the ethnic groups and their languages are more Tibetan and a variant of Buddhism is again common.

Language and power

Controlling, let alone uniting, such a diverse area has been a stiff challenge throughout history. In a country of some 200 languages, divisions and policies are fundamental. The Mughals (see below) made Persian the official language and British traders and administrators used it. This was replaced by English under British rule. At independence, Hindi became the national language of India; in Pakistan, the official language is Urdu, which is spoken like Hindi but written in a Perso-Arabic script. Bangladeshi is different again.

Language issues remain complex, personally and politically. Children in the Himalayan region of Ladakh, part of the Indian province of Jammu-Kashmir, use Ladakhi at primary school, must learn Urdu for all their lessons at secondary school and then master English if they wish to study in higher education. The first constitutional reform of the Indian government after independence was to reshape provincial boundaries to match more closely with linguistic groups.

Religious sensitivities and tensions run through the entire history of British rule and the nationalist campaigns. Hinduism will be considered first as the core culture of India. Islam and Sikhism will be considered in their historical context.

Hindu society

The Hindu religion, the basis of subcontinental society, is one of the oldest in the world. Perhaps because of this, and the importance given to status by birth, Indian society and culture has been described, too loosely, as 'timeless' and 'unchanging'. This is, however, inaccurate and in the analysis which follows, it should be borne in mind that social divisions have always been flexible in reality. On the other hand, this has resulted, arguably, in an even more complex sensitivity to social status, especially as Hinduism has no central authority structure and is managed largely through convention and consensus.

Hinduism is **polytheistic** and highly tolerant (although there are contemporary violent, fundamentalist groups). There are literally numberless gods and goddesses, with continual new additions. Partly because of so much choice and diversity, relationship with a god/dess is less important than public behaviour, termed *dharma*. *Dharma* consists of undertaking religious duties and social responsibilities appropriate to one's religious group. Such groups are called **castes**.

Caste

Caste membership, which is largely defined by birth, determines which occupations may be followed, whom one may marry and even the extent to which one may appear in public.

Classically, there are four castes (termed *varna*): Brahmins, the priests; Kshatriyas, the warriors; Vaishyas, the traders; and Shudras, the cultivators or peasants. Such a schema is not unlike European medieval feudalism but with an explicitly religious basis and function. The respect accorded these groups remains fairly fixed, although actual power might vary from place to place. There are also finer-grained distinctions known as *jatis*, in which social groups fill niches in the labour and occupational structure and whose prestige might rise or fall more quickly. One calculation is that there were over 2000 castes in total.

The persistence of caste into the modern world and its social importance has some bearing on the history of Indian nationalism. In the first place, the Brahmin class, with its sensitivity to respect without power, was a focus for discontent (see Section 2, 'The Indian Mutiny', on page 10) and later for educated resistance and organisation. At the other end of the hierarchy, the oppression of the lowest group, known literally as the Untouchables, became, for Gandhi the nationalist campaigner, part of the need for constitutional reform. Finally, conversion to Islam presented in many ways an attractive escape from the fixities of Hinduism and created areas of Muslim preponderance.

Two other features should be noted: first, most of the regional rulers of India have been Hindus – the Rajahs, Nizams and Nawabs collectively termed the Princes in the British period; and second, the cow is a sacred animal to Hindus, perhaps the most sacred thing of all, and as such vulnerable to offence, leading to outrage and violent reaction.

Key terms

Polytheistic
A religion with many gods and goddesses.

Caste
A rigid public social division. Derived from a Portuguese word.

Mughals, Marathas and Sikhs

Mughals

From the eleventh century, north-western India was raided and invaded by armies, groups and peoples from central Asia, ethnically Turkic. They established a Sultanate at Delhi and consolidated their power. With the accession of Akbar (meaning 'The Great') in 1556, there came to power a dynasty claiming descent from Genghis Khan and Timurlane, near legendary leaders of the Mongol hordes. From this, the dynasty became known as the Mughals (from which comes the English word mogul).

The Mughal civilisation is one of the most brilliant in history. Its cultural achievements are numerous but the Taj Mahal is perhaps the most famous. Politically, the legacy of the Mughal period is of vital importance to the history of independence.

Although Arab Muslims had reached India overland in the seventh century and traded along the coasts, it was the Mughals who established Islam firmly within the subcontinent. They ruled as never more than a minority élite but the prestige attached to Islam ensured that, over time, Muslim culture and individuals were pre-eminent. In the north-west, Muslims were the majority of the general population.

Islam and caste

In the region of Bengal, many people converted to Islam to escape their low status in Hindu caste society. In Islam, as in Hinduism, socio-religious consensus and public behaviour are important. However, Islam places great emphasis on the equality of believers and their direct relationship with one all-powerful god, Allah. This rather more democratic spirit was clearly appealing. As a result, the Bengal area also became one of the majority Muslim regions.

The Mughals held sway over the whole of northern India but were never able to completely dominate the south. The repeated attempts to wage war, requiring constant taxation, eventually wore out the will of both rulers and ruled. From the time of Aurangzeb (d.1707), Mughal power began to decline and territorial control to shrink, although there was still a Mughal Emperor in Delhi in 1858.

Into this situation moved various groups: the Marathas, the Sikhs and the Europeans.

Marathas

The Marathas expanded out of their heartland in the Western Ghats under occasionally brilliant leadership, notably that of Shivaji, in the seventeenth century. Although they eventually brought under their control, directly or indirectly, a huge part of central India, they were unable to unify their various sub-groups into anything more than a loose confederacy of warlords. The relative poverty of their heartland meant that they could not sustain large armies, although when needed huge forces could be put together for set-piece battles. At their height they threatened the European, particularly British, presence right across to Bengal but the challenge provoked a sustained and victorious reaction. The territorial legacy of the Marathas was the major princely state of Hyderabad. The political legacy was a glimpse of all-India rule by Indians. The Marathas are sometimes claimed as a **proto-nationalist** movement.

Key term

Proto-nationalist
A first example or experiment, before adoption of the aims of nationalism.

Sikhs

In the sixteenth century, encouraged to a certain extent by tolerant and multicultural Mughal emperors, religious leaders in the Punjab created a deliberate fusion of Hinduism and Islam, which became known as Sikhism. Amritsar was declared the Sikh holy city after the building of the Golden Temple there. At first, Sikhism was purely a socio-religious innovation. Later Sikh leaders developed a distinctive identity with a militant attitude and military discipline. Over time, the Punjab, one of the most populous regions of the subcontinent, became overwhelmingly Sikh and Muslim with almost no Hindus. For this reason, as we shall see, it was in the Punjab that the most terrible events of partition took place.

The East India Company

Regular English contact with India began in the early 1600s as a result of Elizabeth I granting a charter to the East India Company giving it monopoly trading control of the lucrative spice trade from the Pacific islands of the East Indies, now Indonesia. India itself became an important point to restock food and water on the trading journeys.

Key date

Charter granted to East India Company by Elizabeth I: 1600

The company established bases, literally fortified factories, at three Indian ports, Bombay, Madras and Calcutta, over the same period as the Dutch, French and Portuguese were doing the same. Eventually, the Dutch, at this time a global maritime power, succeeded in ousting other European groups from the islands of the East Indies. So the East India Company (now 'British' as a result of the 1707 Act of Union) was forced to concentrate on expanding its Indian business.

As Mughal power declined and the Marathas sought to exploit opportunities for conquest, the company found itself engaging in defensive warfare to protect its interests. The company created and put into the field its own substantial private army. During the eighteenth century, European wars between Britain and France became global through combat in India and the American colonies. It was in this period that Robert Clive (Clive of India), an unpromising trader as a youth, emerged as a military genius, defeating the equally brilliant French General Dupleix, to become millionaire governor of Bengal.

Corruption and expansion

In the late eighteenth century, service in the East India Company, although 'far from civilisation', was known as a route to personal

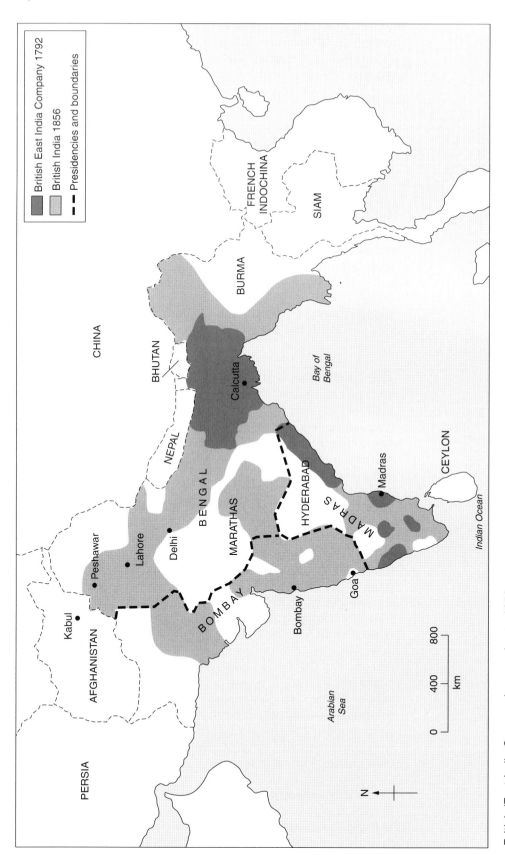

British (East India Company) expansion to 1856.

riches, partly because the company also encouraged private trade and partly because its success over the Marathas and the French meant that it found itself governing ever more area, collecting taxes and running public administration. The company became a by-word for corruption, culminating in the impeachment, that is trial in the House of Commons itself, of Warren Hastings, the governor-general.

Aggressive expansion resulted in the British control of the entire Gangetic plain as far as the Sutlej river by 1818. Nevertheless, the company professed to have no political objectives. It was simply trying to protect trade and capture (literally) more market.

The administration of the company was divided into three presidencies, based at Calcutta, Bombay and Madras. In 1833, the post of governor-general of Fort William, Calcutta, became the concurrent governor-general of India.

One ironic footnote to this period is that the French, Dutch and Portuguese all retained ownership of various port-cities, such as Pondicherry, Cochin and Goa, not just through the period of British rule but beyond independence. They were only finally handed back to India in the 1950s.

Intervention

From 1820 the British saw themselves clearly as the dominant power in India for the foreseeable future. However, military success, territorial acquisition and administrative competence led only to larger questions, perhaps partly born of self-confidence, partly something more like conscience: what was the point of controlling India, what to do with it, where was it going? Increasingly, their attitude displayed a paternalistic concern to spread the benefits of British civilisation and Christian culture. This attitude was to become known, at the height of empire, as the **White Man's Burden** – difficult and unrewarding work but someone's got to do it.

An early example was the criminalisation and consequent suppression of *sati* (or *suttee*). *Sati* was the Hindu custom, following the death of any notable Hindu male, which required his widow to throw herself voluntarily upon the funeral pyre to be burned alive. It was commonly known that, in the event of natural reluctance, families would pressurise grief-stricken widows to comply and, failing that, take matters into their own hands. The British (that is the company) outlawed *sati* in 1829. Although there is evidence to suggest that the suppression of this custom was privately welcomed, it nevertheless marked a public precedent of interference in Hindu socio-religious affairs.

Less controversial was the suppression of *thuggee* (from which the English word 'thug' derives). Hindu devotees of the goddess Kali believed that their cult demanded human sacrifice and procured this through the strangulation of random victims. Suppression took rather longer to achieve than with *sati* but was largely complete by 1837.

White Man's Burden
The perceived duty to govern so-called inferior races and countries.

A further manifestation was the **minute** on education prepared in 1835 by Thomas Babington Macaulay, member of the governor-general's supreme council of India, which declared the intention of establishing and developing an education system throughout India.

Technological benefits of European civilisation, such as railways and telegraph communication, were introduced in the name of progress but without realising the anxieties and resentments they might be stoking up.

Finally, under the governor-generalship of Lord Dalhousie (1848–56), a controversial policy of **annexation** was implemented. If the ruler of a (Hindu) state or province died without a son to inherit power, then the province was simply declared part of British territory. This legal device resulted in the addition of huge areas to British possessions.

Key terms

Minute
An official document.

Annexation
Forced but peaceful conquest of territory.

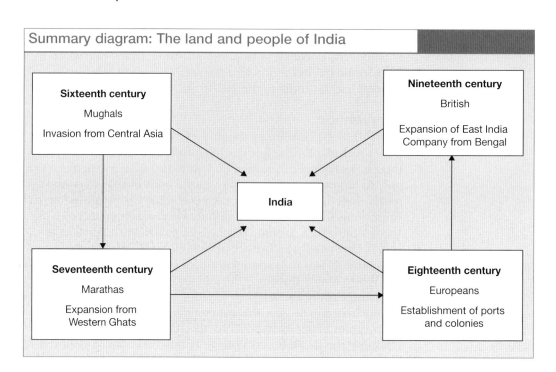

Summary diagram: The land and people of India

Sixteenth century

Mughals

Invasion from Central Asia

Nineteenth century

British

Expansion of East India Company from Bengal

India

Seventeenth century

Marathas

Expansion from Western Ghats

Eighteenth century

Europeans

Establishment of ports and colonies

2 | The Indian Mutiny 1857

Matters came to a head in 1857. What came to be known as the Indian Mutiny left a deep psychological scar. What happened was terrible; the thought of what might have happened – and might still happen – lurked in the collective British memory for the rest of British rule right up to the Second World War.

Indian Mutiny: 1857

Key date

Causes

The key causes of the mutiny were a mixture of political grievance and religious fears.

Politically, the policy of annexing princely states without immediate heirs into British control had created widespread

Key question
Why did the mutiny happen?

resentment and anxieties, not least because it threw out of employment large numbers of advisers to the princes.

This was combined with religious anxieties which had been completely overlooked. The prestigious Brahmin caste viewed the new railways with horror. They feared religious pollution by coming into contact, literally, with Untouchables in railway carriages and stations.

Moreover, Brahmins formed a large proportion of **sepoys** in the army and recent declarations had made it clear that army regiments might be deployed outside their home region and even overseas. To the Brahmin caste, a sea voyage results in a huge loss of caste respect.

It only needed one final spark to ignite rebellion. Sepoys were outraged by rumours that newly issued cartridges for their rifles had been greased for easier loading (which also involved tearing off part of the cartridge with the mouth) with either beef fat, sacred to Hindus, or pork fat, prohibited by Islam. As one writer has put it 'with amazing insensitivity both were true'.

Key events
The key events were:

• The British court-martialled and humiliated 85 sepoys at the barracks in Meerut, near Delhi, for refusing to use the cartridges. They were freed by mutineers the same night who

A contemporary engraving of Miss Ulrica Wheeler (aged 18 years) defending herself during the Indian Mutiny published in a popular book. What feelings might this arouse in British readers? Miss Wheeler was popularly thought to have been killed or killed herself. There is strong evidence that she lived a full but disguised life as the Muslim wife of one of her attackers or rescuers.

then massacred all local Europeans, including women and children.

- The rapid spread of mutiny throughout the Bengal Army of northern India, although the other two armies – of Bombay and Madras – remained calm and loyal, as did the Sikhs of the Punjab and the princely states. The entire Gangetic plain was soon out of British control.

- The mutineers marched to Delhi to proclaim the 82-year-old Mughal Emperor ruler of all India. This led to peasant uprisings. Local leaders emerged at the head of anti-British forces. Notable examples were the Nana Sahib of Oudh and the (female) Rani of Jhansi who dressed as a Maratha princess-rebel, died in battle and was described by one contemporary Briton as 'the only man among the rebels'.

- At Cawnpore in the particularly volatile province of Oudh, 400 British men, women and children surrendered to mutineers and were offered safe passage on boats. On their way to the boats they were massacred; 200 others were saved, possibly as future hostages against the advancing British troops, but were then killed by butchers since the mutineers refused to carry out the killings in cold blood.

- At Lucknow, some 3000 troops and civilian families endured a five-month siege by mutineers. They feared the worst, as did the British public reading regular dispatches in the newspapers (see picture), but were eventually rescued by the largest British, that is non-sepoy, army put together on the subcontinent. If Cawnpore represented Britain at its most vulnerable, Lucknow was seen as a sign of ultimate indomitability.

Consequences

The immediate military consequences were that:

- British reprisals were vicious and deliberately designed to strike terror into the peasant population. Entire villages suspected of support for mutineers were massacred by the British. At Cawnpore itself, mutineers and others were forced to try to lick clean the blood-stained buildings, before being made to eat pork or beef and then publicly hanged. Elsewhere, mutineers were loaded into cannons and literally blown to bits.

- The proportion of Indian sepoys in the army was reduced by 40 per cent and British troops increased by 50 per cent so that the ratio became 3:1 rather than 9:1.

- Recruitment of sepoys switched from prestigious Hindu Brahmin and Rajput castes to the more loyal areas of the Sikh Punjab and the Muslim north-west. It was ensured that adjacent regiments had different ethnic and religious backgrounds.

- Troops were allowed to use whatever grease they preferred and in 1867 the breech-loading rifle made this type of cartridge obsolete.

Key question
What were the effects of the mutiny?

A contemporary engraving of mutineers being blown to pieces by cannons. What might be the relationship between the chosen punishment, visual representation and popular feeling?

- In 1869, the opening of the Suez Canal and in 1870 the completion of a telegraph system overland to Britain made reinforcement a quicker prospect if needed.

Key debate: mutiny or rebellion?

The British attempted, largely successfully at the time, to represent the events as either a disaster in which they were merely victims or, at worst, a military phenomenon. By emphasising the term 'Indian Mutiny' they tried to calm fears by focusing the problem so that solutions could be identified. In the short term, certain military individuals became **scapegoats** on the grounds of indecisiveness. This myth of delayed response was, however, to have even more devastating consequences in the Amritsar Massacre of 1919.

It is clear, however, that it was more than a mutiny and to some extent this was recognised at the time. It was not expressed openly so that the significant cultural, political and constitutional consequences which followed could be presented as high-minded gifts rather than fearful rewards. They heralded a new era for the British in India and for Indian nationalism.

From this perspective, events are more accurately described today as, for example, the Great Rebellion. Some nationalist and Muslim historians even have claimed it was a national **insurgency** or (failed) war of independence.

Key terms

Scapegoat
A person chosen to carry the blame for others.

Insurgency
A prolonged uprising.

Key dates

Crown control of India: 1858

Amritsar Massacre: 1919

Summary diagram: The Indian Mutiny 1857

Causes	Effects
• Fear of Christian missionary activity • Interventions in socio-religious customs • Fear of caste pollution through travel and transport • Annexation of territories, loss of jobs • Offence at pork- and beef-greased cartridges	• Abolition of East India Company • Parliament control • Royal proclamation of protection of religious freedom • Reward princes and landowners • Develop education system and open jobs to Indians • Develop transport and communications, reduce proportion of sepoys in army, avoid high-caste recruitment

3 | Raj and Renaissance

A new beginning: crown control

In the aftermath of the rebellion the British were determined to bring the administration of India under closer government control. First, the East India Company was abolished. That was a relatively simple matter of putting the British house in order. Second, the Mughal Empire was brought to an end. The aged Emperor was given a pension and sent into exile in Burma, with little regret on either his part or others. Third, the British monarch, then Queen Victoria, was declared the ruler of India. As a consequence, the British government took over direct control of the former East India Company territories and began a series of robust treaty negotiations with the Indian princes to bring them under indirect control.

In recognition of crown control, the governor-general now also took the title of **viceroy**. The viceroy was accountable to Parliament through a secretary of state for India and an India council.

It was recognised that the government must keep in touch with Indian public opinion, both in its own territories and in the princely states. As the first of a series of cautious measures to involve Indians in government, the Legislative Council in India now included Indian advisers, appointed by the viceroy.

In the princely states, a twin-track approach was adopted. The hard line was that the states were pressured into recognising that their independence was preserved and protected by the dominance of British power and that they should do nothing to challenge that. The more supportive line was investment in education and training in their states, although this did not last long. Of more interest to the princes was the establishment of an elaborate hierarchy of honours and privileges, including the number of guns permitted to fire in salute on state occasions. The Star of India was the supreme award to favoured rulers.

Key question
Why and how did the British re-order their government of India?

Viceroy
The deputy for a monarch.

Key term

Key dates

Royal Proclamation:
1858

Queen Victoria
declared Empress:
1877

Victoria

There was considerable warmth in the relationship between Queen Victoria and India. Indians broadly welcomed direct, if distant, rule. Victoria herself maintained a special affection for India and, in later life, kept an Indian personal adviser in her household, Abdul Karim.

The origin of this mutual admiration lies in the famous Royal Proclamation of 1858, deliberately written by Viscount Canning, the first viceroy, to suggest personal respect for Indians and interest in their advancement.

After stating respect for 'the rights, dignity and honour of native Princes as our own …' and disclaiming any desire to extend British territory, the key statement was:

> … it is our further will that, so far as may be, our subjects, of whatever race or creed, be freely and impartially admitted to offices in our service, the duties of which they may be qualified, by their education, ability, and integrity, duly to discharge.

This part of the proclamation was interpreted by the British as a policy to develop, cautiously, the involvement of Indians at all levels in the administration. On the Indian side, it would come to be seen as laying the foundations for self-government. However, at this time independence was not envisaged for the foreseeable future, not least because educated Indians regarded British rule as helpful to the social and economic development of India itself.

In 1877 the special relationship was further acknowledged by a proclamation that the Queen was now also Empress of India in particular.

Religion

It was widely recognised that religious sensitivities had played a major part in the causes of the rebellion. There were not only threats to the particular requirements of **indigenous** Hindu and Muslim practice, but also a general resentment of missionary activity, including widespread fears of compulsory conversion to Christianity.

Accordingly, the proclamation also set out policy on religious intervention:

Key term

Indigenous
People native to a
place (but not
primitive).

> We disclaim alike the right and desire to impose our [Christian] convictions on any of our subjects. We declare it to be our royal will and pleasure that none be in anywise favoured, none molested or disquieted, by reason of their religious faith or observances, but that all alike shall enjoy the equal and impartial protection of the law and we do strictly charge and enjoin all those who may be in authority under us that they abstain from all interference with the religious belief or worship of any of our subjects on pain of our highest displeasure.

It has been argued that this also laid the foundations for demands in the nationalist movement for recognition of separate political rights for different religious communities. This in turn became the demand for partition into separate nations based on religious preference.

Indian social renaissance

The second half of the nineteenth century is often regarded as the zenith of the British Raj. In fact, the British ceased to acquire territory and intervened less than before, certainly in moral or religious matters. They turned instead to less controversial social projects, dubbed 'trains and drains' by modern historian John Keay since it involved large-scale irrigation projects to increase food production and avert famines. At the same time, there was a growth in **secular** education and in intellectual and cultural debate. Conscious attempts were made to modernise religious attitudes among both Hindus and Indian Muslims. There was a growing sense of India as a nation in the making. This provided the necessary conditions in which nationalist ideas and campaigns could grow.

As the viceroy, Lord Ripon, explained:

> We cannot now rely upon military force alone and policy as well as justice ought to prompt us to endeavour to govern more and more by means of and in accordance with that growing public opinion which is beginning to show itself throughout the country.
>
> We shall not subvert the British Empire by allowing the Bengali baboo [*babu*] to discuss his own schools and drains. Rather shall we afford him a safety-valve if we can turn his attention to such innocuous subjects.

Three British projects, in particular, were significant to the development of nationalist movements.

Entry to the Indian Civil Service

First, the terms of Victoria's proclamation were honoured and jobs in government were opened to Indian applicants. The Indian Civil Service (ICS), which had been in effect a branch of the East India Company, was turned into an efficient organisation actually to run government in India. Entry to the ICS was by examination (although only since 1853) and educated Indians were now free to apply. There were two slight snags: there was very little education in India itself and the examinations were held in Britain. The costs of overcoming these barriers were beyond the overwhelming majority of Indian families. According to one historian, only 12 Indians had entered the ICS through open examination by 1887. As a consequence of growing resentment, the examinations were switched to India in the 1890s but by 1913 Indians were only 5 per cent of the ICS.

Key terms

Renaissance
A rebirth or flowering of culture.

Secular
Public, non-religious affairs.

Babu
Bengali term for clerk.

Investment in education

Second, and partly as a result of the recognition of these barriers, there was a drive to increase education at all levels. Some higher education had existed in the Bengal area. There was now investment, not so much to provide the education, but to support local initiatives. Progress was slow and it should be noted that it was not until 1870 that comprehensive primary education was established in Britain itself. However, there was huge expansion of higher educational opportunity and the lower levels of bureaucracy were filled with Indian civil servants, matched by a slow withdrawal of Britons willing to work in the same grades. The growth of education in the English language and of professional employment gradually created an Indian middle class which was to become the fertile soil of the nationalist movement.

Communications and transport

The third area of progress was in communications and transport. Notwithstanding the caste sensitivities noted above, the railway network expanded relentlessly, partly for military and governmental reasons, partly to stimulate trade and economy and partly to prepare for the transportation of foodstuffs in the likelihood of failed monsoons and regional famines. Similarly, the modernisation of the Great Trunk Road linking Calcutta with the Punjab along the towns of the Gangetic plain was a major project.

Along with a growing telegraph network, the railways permitted the circulation across the whole of India of English-language newspapers, the number of which was also expanding through use of technology and the growth of the middle class. This in turn fed a growing sense of national consciousness over and above the historic regionalism created by geography and linguistic divisions.

Growing trade with Britain in both export of raw materials (cotton, jute, rice, tea) and import of manufactured goods (cotton, steel, engineering) also helped create an international outlook and connections with global, albeit imperialist, economies.

Key question
How did Muslim regeneration lead eventually to partition?

Key dates

Foundation of Aligarh College: 1875

Ilbert Bill: 1883

The Aligarh movement

Leading Indians also took steps to regenerate society through education and modernisation. The aim was to create a Westernised intellectual class, and increase both Indian self-respect and British confidence by the adoption of cooperative and forward-looking ideas amongst Indians. This was particularly true of the Muslim community which still felt blamed for the Mutiny.

In 1875, Sir Syed Ahmed Khan founded the Muslim Anglo-Oriental College. Besides education in Islamic studies and the Urdu language, much emphasis was placed on studying Western science, literature and history. In 1913, it became a full university.

The location of Aligarh College gave its name to a broad movement across India with the aim of increasing Muslim prominence in social affairs. Although Khan supported a general unity of Hindus and Muslims, the movement also initiated the idea of two self-respecting communal nations within India.

The Aligarh movement rejected involvement in any agitation and members were told not to join the Congress Party after its formation in 1885 (see below). However, this was as much because there was also a determination to secure special political representation for Muslims. This led to the formation of a political organisation (party), the All-India Muslim League in 1906 (see below). The Muslim League would eventually become, under its final leader, Muhammad Ali Jinnah, the driving force for partition and the creation of Muslim Pakistan.

The Ilbert Bill

Even as the British and Indians were jointly bringing into existence an educated middle class, almost without noticing, the British were withdrawing as a social group. They held themselves aloof from the new India, particularly as it became more interested in politics. Whereas the employees of the East India Company lived alongside Indians, to the extent that many had Indian wives and mistresses, the imperial Britons shunned contact. It has been be said that the British turned themselves into an ultra-caste, with their own various *jatis* of status marked by title, residence, social peers and activity. They became increasingly obsessed with their own affairs, particularly in the hot season when almost the entire British class moved up into the cooler hill towns and the summer capital of Simla (*Shimla*).

This attitude was seen in practice in 1883 with the reaction to the so-called Ilbert Bill. The bill was a rational consequence of increasing numbers of Indians entering the legal profession and the judiciary, as qualified and experienced as any Briton. It proposed that at lower levels, the jurisdiction of the courts should be applied equally to Britons and Indians. There was little initial reaction to the measure when put in such abstract terms.

Reaction of Europeans

As soon as it was realised that, in practice, this meant that white Britons would be tried by Indian judges there was uproar.

In some way there returned the mutiny fear that white British women would be left to the mercies of local males, who had done nothing to protect their own womenfolk from the terrors of *sati*, for example.

The British made it clear that they would refuse to obey the law if passed and the proposal was amended to preserve discrimination so that all-white juries would reach the verdict on white defendants.

The effect of this so-called 'white mutiny' on educated Indian opinion was two-fold. First, there was increased pessimism that the British would ever really respect Indians, let alone give them responsibility and power. This created more support for nationalist ideas as they began to develop. Second, the success of threatened widespread passive resistance to the rule of law was noted for future reference, not least perhaps by Mohandas Gandhi, aged 14 years at the time, but shortly to become a lawyer

> **Key question**
> How did the Europeans in India react to the Ilbert Bill?

and subsequently the greatest exponent of non-violent resistance in history.

The formation of Congress

Key dates

Formation of
Congress Party: 1885

Indian Councils Act:
1892

Key terms

Congress
A meeting.

Durbar
Imperial
celebration.

Sabha
An association.

Although it would be tempting to see the formation of the Indian National **Congress** in 1885 as a response to the Ilbert Bill, its origins have been discerned in the imperial **durbar** of January 1877. The leaders of the Pune Sarvajanik *Sabha* published an open letter to the princes, chiefs and gentlemen invited to the durbar of which the following is a key passage:

> The gathering of so many representative men from all parts of India is an event of national importance … the commencement of that fusion of races and creeds, the second birth of the great Indian nation. You are the great Notables of the land, the first Parliament of the united Indian nation, the first Congress of the representatives of [its] diverse states and nationalities … We propose … that you will all meet together in private gatherings and discuss with each other our present situation and future prospects.

The first Congresses were indeed more like educational meetings than political conferences. In due course, however, Congress, as it quickly became known, would become a recognisable political party and the driving force for nationalism and full independence over the next 50 years.

Perhaps strange to relate, therefore, that its founder was a Scot, Allan Octavian Hume; perhaps not, given that the early years of Congress saw it arguing for only slight concessions from the British Raj which it generally regarded as a good thing for India.

The Indian Councils Act

One such concession was the 1892 Indian Councils Act which modestly increased the number of Indians on local councils.

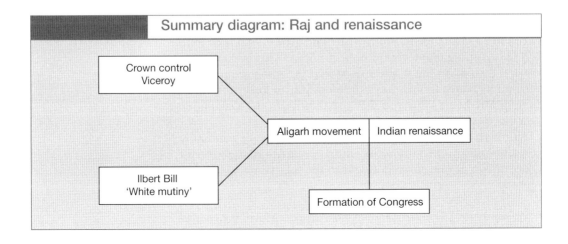

Summary diagram: Raj and renaissance

4 | Imperialism and Nationalism

Imperialist attitudes

In the late nineteenth century the British Empire was the largest in world history. It was, however, but one of a number of European empires then at their height. The French, Belgians, Germans and Italians together with the British had all scrambled for parts of Africa and nearer to home the Austro-Hungarian and **Ottoman Empires** remained solid. All had difficulties with local peoples and politics, but there was no sense that imperialism as a global system would disappear. However, history taught the lesson of inexorable decline and fall and many South American countries had gained independence from Spain in the nineteenth century itself.

Official British policy was commitment to eventual Indian self-government within the Empire. There was no sense that independence would ever be a goal of British policy and even self-government was seen publicly as a lengthy project of many decades. Empires were costly to run but they provided easy colonial markets for goods manufactured in the European home countries to the benefit of the home economy.

Privately, as revealed in contemporary correspondence and later memoirs, most British leaders and officials desired the process of political development to be so drawn out as to be without a date. The sheer size and symbolism of India as a 'possession' of the British made it indispensable to the British power across the globe. In addition, the Indian Army was a huge military force at its disposal in Asia. Figures such as Viceroy Curzon and Winston Churchill, later prime minister, openly declared that without India, Britain would be a second- or third-rate power.

Socially, the British shouldered willingly the so-called white man's burden of passing on and nurturing European culture and civilisation. Such a responsibility was of course self-defined and self-justifying. One British leader described it, perhaps tastelessly, as 'splendid happy slavery'. In practice, however, it did mean the development of at least an educated élite which was, by 1900, becoming a challenge to the British. The growth of a *babu* élite was outstripping employment opportunities. This of course created discontent but it also meant that the same group had time on its hands to imagine a different way of governing India. In addition, being educated they used letters to the newspapers as a way of sharing ideas and complaints.

Although this might be seen as one of the roots of nationalist consciousness in the twentieth century, in fact thinking was still cooperative. As one correspondent to the Kesari newspaper wrote (quoted in Mehrotra, 1978):

> We are thoroughly convinced that India cannot recover her national freedom in the real sense of the word independently of English protection, assistance and control. We are aware of the loss which we are at present suffering from British government yet we do not

Key question
What was the attitude to independence?

Ottoman Empire
Islamic Empire of the Middle East and modern Turkey.

Key term

believe that our condition will be any better by the exchange of the British rule for that of any other nation … Since we are not in a position to gain our independence by fighting with the English or to preserve it when gained it is desirable that we should advance step by step behaving in a conciliatory manner with the British.

Moreover, all parties had taken notice of the defeat in 1886 of the bill to provide home rule for Ireland. On the one hand, if the oldest British colony was not to be granted movement towards independence then there was no hope for India; on the other, perhaps Ireland was too close for comfort and India might pose a more persuasive case of difference.

In short, perhaps the most that could be hoped for, sooner or later, was that India would gain **dominion status** within the Empire. Dominion status had been granted to Canada in 1867 (and Australia was scheduled for 1901). For India, the key question was whether India was yet a nation. Many certainly spoke of it as a nation in the making. But the fact that today many consider it to be still a nation in the making only reinforces the view that, in 1900, many considered there to be some doubt about ever unifying India under Indian rule.

As a twentieth-century Indian politician, Chandra Pal, commented (quoted in Brown, 1994):

Our language has no word corresponding to the English word nation … And the reason is that our social synthesis practically stopped with the race-idea.

British India

The governance of British India retained the structure of the settlement in the aftermath of the great rebellion of 1857 as set out in Figure 1.1.

The peoples of Britain and British India alike were subjects of the crown. The monarch was head of state and emperor/empress of India in particular. In common conception, this figurehead was supreme although constitutionally the king or queen was the crown *in* Parliament.

Responsibility for Indian affairs rested with the secretary of state for India, a member of the cabinet and accountable to Parliament, who was advised by the India Council.

In India itself, the viceroy was supreme, the representative of the monarch but appointed by the prime minister and accountable to the secretary of state. The personal and political relationship of these two post-holders – viceroy and secretary of state – was crucial to the initiation, or otherwise, of constitutional and political developments in and for India. Key reforms in the twentieth century are often known by the joint names of the respective leaders.

Although technological progress meant that by 1900 telegraphic communication between London and India was relatively quick and easy, the viceroy had considerable powers of delegated government and, in states of emergency, absolute

Key term

Dominion status
A category of self-government within the British Empire denoting a full nation.

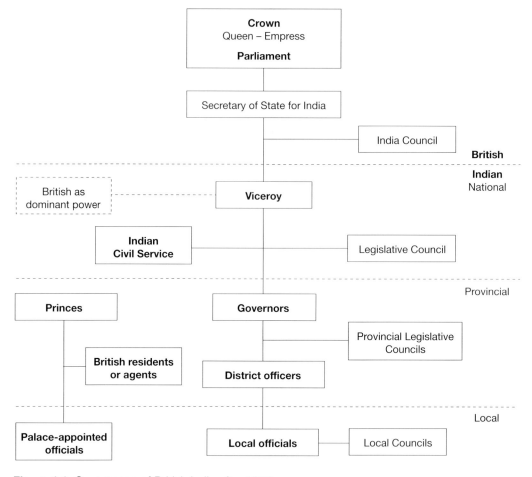

Figure 1.1: Governance of British India after 1857.

power. (This power was carried over into the independent period and exercised for considerable periods in both India and Pakistan.)

The viceroy had a military commander-in-chief in India, overseeing the three armies still based on the presidencies of the East India Company, and was advised by a national Legislative Council, overwhelmingly composed of British officials.

The 11 British provinces (unchanged since 1857) had governors, advised by provincial councils, although only certain matters were permitted for discussion and decision.

The princely states

In 1900, many areas of the subcontinent were still not ruled directly by the British. About one-fifth of the population, 72 million people, were the subjects of the 561 Indian rulers, with various titles such as Rajah, Nawab or Nizam, known collectively as the Indian princes.

The princes ruled nominally independent states (originally styled native states and then princely states), which varied

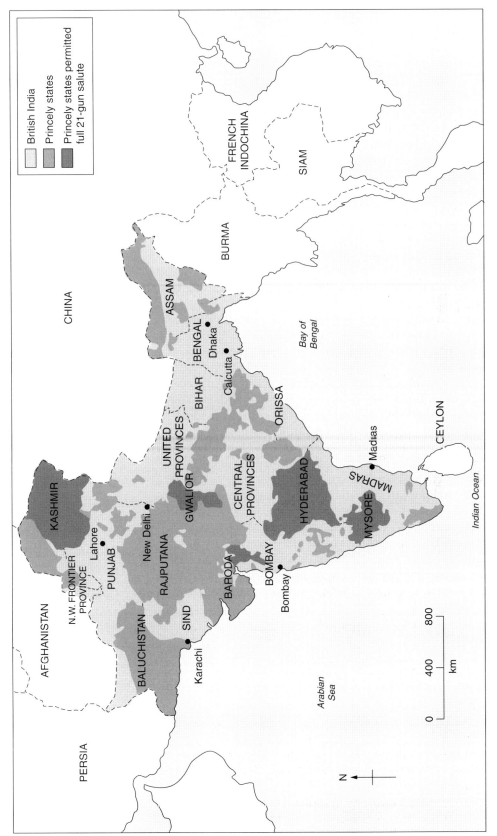

India c.1900 showing British provinces and major princely states.

considerably in size. Some states, such as Hyderabad in the south or Jammu and Kashmir in the north-west (c. 200,000 km^2 each), were larger than Britain itself. Others were so small they were more like country estates and could not be found on maps.

Paramountcy and oversight

After the mutiny, the British stopped acquiring territory either by military force or by political annexation. They permitted the Indian princes to continue to rule, partly as a reward for loyalty during the mutiny and partly to save more direct expense by the government. Moreover, they established formal honours to flatter the princes.

On the other hand, the princely states were forced to acknowledge Britain as the **paramount power** within the subcontinent. This too was typically sweetened as a treaty guaranteeing British military protection. However, the British reserved, and sometimes exercised, the right to remove a prince found to be working against the British interest or causing trouble with neighbouring princes.

In order to monitor princely politics, a British official was placed in the royal court. In the larger states, such an official was known as the resident. Smaller states received visits from a **peripatetic** agent.

Sati, female infanticide and slavery were practised in some princely states without British intervention in accordance with post-rebellion policy. More attention was paid to persuading princes to reduce their armed forces. Military intervention was found necessary in some cases, for example in Manipur in 1891, resulting in executions of officials, exile of princes and appointment of alternative rulers.

However, in line with educational policy, rulers were encouraged to establish colleges for the education of their sons in the British public school mould. Some acquired the taste for European style and used their wealth to live it up in Britain. Although this caused concern about possible resentment among the population, of still more concern to the British were rulers who were so progressive that they veered towards nationalist sentiments.

Communal India

Running through the old India of the princely states and the new order of British India was the third, **communal** India of national and international religions, of linguistic divisions and of regional consciousness.

Hindus

Hinduism had undergone a revival in the second half of the nineteenth century as part of the social and cultural renaissance. Pride and sensitivity had increased to the extent that in many provinces the protection of **sacred cows** was the major political issue. This in turn offered more opportunity to those determined to cause offence and stir up inter-religious communal violence.

Key terms

Paramount power
A diplomatic term for the most powerful force, often an occupying army.

Peripatetic
Moving round from one workplace to another.

Communal
Relating to a religious community across the whole population.

Sacred cow
In Hinduism actual cows are sacred; the term is widely used to indicate a protected idea.

At the same time, a more intellectual and spiritual interest had grown to match the stirrings of nationalism. For a long time being a Hindu mostly involved general social behaviour but it now became normal to talk of Hinduism as a self-conscious faith. This fusion of modernisation and of traditionalism took on the name **Sanskritisation**.

Muslims

Muslims observed a growing Hindu assertiveness with concern. Hitherto, as long as their customs could be practised unhindered, Hindu society had seemed content to live under another's regime. This had been the basis of stable Mughal rule for many years. Now they feared the boot would be on the other foot. During the 1890s Muslim defence associations were formed.

The decline and fall of Mughal power remained not just a historical disappointment, but a real personal problem of politics and religion. The religion of Islam obliged Muslims to work for the political dominance of Islam or to move to an existing Islamic country. In addition, Muslims owed an allegiance to the **Khalifah**, in the person of the reigning Sultan of Turkey. This international political dimension to the community of Islam was viewed with suspicion. As a result of all this, subcontinental Muslims remained undecided about committing to Indian nationalism.

Sikhs

Amidst this religious sensitivity, the Sikhs too felt anxious. The Sikhs were clustered in the province of the Punjab along with roughly equal numbers of Muslims. To the north-west, the provinces were overwhelmingly Muslim, the south-east was overwhelmingly Hindu, the northern provinces of the Gangetic plain were fairly mixed whereas parts of Bengal were again predominantly Muslim.

Key terms

Sanskrit
An ancient Indian language.

Khalifah
Deputy of the founder of Islam, sometimes caliph.

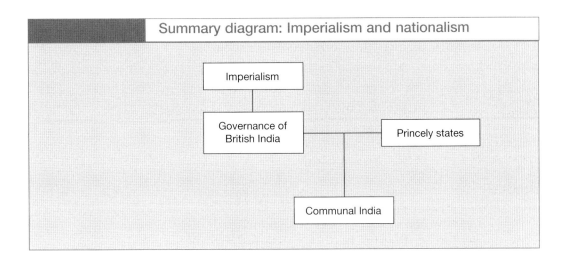

Summary diagram: Imperialism and nationalism

The key debate: historiography

There are two broad approaches in the historiography of Indian independence. Books intended for a commercial British market focus on British rule and conclude with the business of endings and departures. Independence is granted and power is handed over but there is also to some extent an implication of mismanagement and failure, an air of accusation and justification. Nevertheless, this view of the British in India is in harmony with an enduring popular fascination with the culture of the subcontinent, ranging from restaurants through tourism to music and film.

Less widely available are books which focus on the continuity and integrity of the development of the nationalist aspiration and campaigns. This view of India is a matter of rights, demands and struggle, culminating in success and a new beginning. While there are many detailed and scholarly texts, one should be wary of an explicitly nationalist approach to the independence movement, particularly on non-authoritative websites.

A crucial aspect of the historiography is the treatment of Muslim campaigns and the Pakistan movement. Generally speaking, the desire to keep India together is regarded as honourable if not entirely realistic. By contrast, Muslim demands are sometimes presented as a late feature with implications of opportunism, inconsistency or even perversity. Jinnah is subtly presented as an obstructive and manipulative character, almost a villain, whereas Gandhi and Nehru are presented as determined and politically adept even when adopting the same tactics as Jinnah.

Through this book the continuity of Muslim concerns and their relationship to the tactics of the Congress Party and concessions by the British government will be explored. A key judgement to be made is whether the British sympathised with the Muslim demands or whether these demands were used to split the nationalist movement. Such a policy when used by a dominant power is termed '**divide and rule**'.

Divide and rule Imperialist strategy, from Romans onward, of provoking enmities to prevent subject groups uniting in opposition.

Key term

Some key books in the debate
Histories
A.C. Banerjee, *The Constitutional History of India* (in three volumes) (Macmillan, 1978).
J. Brown, *Modern India* (Oxford University Press, 1994).
T. Coates (ed.), *The Amritsar Massacre* (Stationery Office, 2000).
L. Collins and D. Lapierre, *Freedom at Midnight* (HarperCollins, 1997).
P. French, *Liberty or Death* (Flamingo 1998).
H.V. Hodson, *The Great Divide* (Oxford University Press, 1985).
L. James, *Raj* (Little Brown, 1997).
C. Markovits, *A History of Modern India 1480–1950* (Anthem, 2004).
P. Mehra, *A Dictionary of Modern Indian History, 1707–1947* (Oxford University Press, 1987).
S.R. Mehrotra, *Towards India's Freedom* (Vikas, 1978).
P. Robb, *A History of India* (Palgrave, 2002).
P. Shankar Jha, *Kashmir 1947* (Oxford University Press, 1996).
S. Wolpert, *Shameful Flight* (Oxford University Press, 2006).

Biographies, Memoirs and Anthologies
A.S. Ahmed, *Jinnah, Pakistan and the Search for Saladin* (Routledge, 1997).
M.J. Akbar, *Nehru: The Making of India* (Viking Penguin, 1988).
U. Butalia, *The Other Side of Silence* (Hurst, 2000).
L. Fischer, *The Essential Gandhi* (Vintage, 1983).
B. Parekh, *Gandhi, A Very Short Introduction* (Oxford, 1997).
S. Taroor, *Nehru, the Invention of India* (Arcade, 2005).
S. Wolpert, *Jinnah of Pakistan* (Oxford University Press, 1989).

Study Guide: AS Questions

In the style of Edexcel

Source 1

From: a letter sent from Queen Victoria to Prime Minister Lord Salisbury, at the end of the nineteenth century.

The viceroy must hear for himself what the feelings of the natives really are, and do what he thinks right if we are to go on peaceably and happily in India, and to be liked and beloved by high and low. And not try to trample on the people, continually reminding them and making them feel that they are a conquered people.

Source 2

From: a letter to a Kesari newspaper in 1900 quoted in S.R. Mehrotra, Towards India's Freedom, *published in 1978.*

We do not believe our condition will be any better by the exchange of the British rule for that of any other nation. Since we are not in a position to gain our independence by fighting with the English, it is desirable that we should advance step by step behaving in a conciliatory manner with the British.

Source 3

A photograph of part of the great procession of the Indian princes at the Delhi Durbar in 1903. This occasion was organised by the viceroy, Lord Curzon, for the princes to acknowledge the Coronation of Edward VII.

Use Sources 1, 2 and 3 and your own knowledge.
How far do these sources suggest that British rule was accepted in India at the beginning of the twentieth century? Explain your answer, using the evidence of Sources 1, 2 and 3.   (20 marks)

Exam tips

This is an example of your first question, which is compulsory. It is a short-answer question, and you should not write more than three or four paragraphs. Note that you are required to reach a judgement on the evidence of these sources only. The question does not ask you to write what you know about attitudes to British Rule in India in the early twentieth century. However, you should apply your own knowledge to the sources when you use them. For example, in the case of Source 1, you should be aware of the role of a viceroy, and so the examiners will not explain that to you. More importantly, your own knowledge of Queen Victoria's position will enable you to see her instructions and concerns as knowledgeable and authoritative and you should bear that in mind when you use the content of Source 1.

  When you deal with a visual source, such as Source 3, do not just concentrate on describing what you can see. Instead, think about what the details suggest or imply. From Source 3 you can see a huge occasion, the attendance of huge crowds, the richly decorated carriages carried by the many elephants. What does all that suggest? You have evidence of the acknowledgement and celebration of the coronation with great splendour. On the other hand, since this was organised by the viceroy, it is part of a process to promote and cement acceptance of British rule as well as evidence of its acceptance.

   When you deal with these types of questions you are weighing up the evidence. Bear in mind that the evidence of the sources you are given will point in different directions. So, in this case, you will know immediately that there is some evidence suggesting acceptance of British rule and some evidence challenging that. First, sort points from the sources into two columns according to whether they suggest acceptance or questioning of British rule. Source 1 shows the queen to be sensitive to the feelings of the people, but her concerns could suggest that there is some evidence of resentment. How could you use the source content to support both those points? How can Source 2 be used similarly to show both questioning, and acceptance of, British rule?

   After you have placed evidence on both sides, ask yourself whether there is more weight on one side. Having considered each of the sources, try to group points from them together and then come to a conclusion.

2 Discontent to Outrage 1901–19

POINTS TO CONSIDER
In the period 1901–19, Indians began to see the British in a new light. The idea that the British were a civilising authority was seriously damaged by a high-handed viceroy, Lord Curzon, by the bloodbath of the First World War and by the Amritsar Massacre in 1919.

Liberal Party governments in Britain passed legislation to involve more Indians in the administration of India. However, there were also more organised political movements in India.

This chapter examines in more detail:

- Political reorganisation made by the British, notably the Partition of Bengal
- Indian political campaigns, splits and agreements
- The effect of the First World War and the Amritsar Massacre
- Major political concession and reform by the British

Key dates

1901		North West Frontier Province created
1905		Russia defeated by Japan
	October 16	Partition of Bengal
	December	Liberal government
1906	October	Simla delegation
	December	All-India Muslim League formed
1907		Congress split at Surat
1909		Indian Councils Act
1911		Bengal reunited and Delhi became British capital
1914		Outbreak of the First World War
1916		Formation of home rule leagues
		Lucknow Pact
1917	August 20	Montagu Declaration
1918		End of the First World War
		US President Wilson's Fourteen Points
1919		Rowlatt Act
	April 13	Amritsar Massacre
	December	Government of India Act

1 | Reorganisation

Curzon

Key question
What did Curzon
want to achieve?

At the dawn of the twentieth century, the Viceroy of India, Lord Curzon, regarded his purpose as preserving India for the British Empire forever. History, however, regards his two successive terms of office as high noon for the Raj. Had Curzon retired after the durbar of 1903, his reputation, even as a dedicated imperialist, might have been safe. But he was then only 47 years old and accepted a second term of office without self-doubt. The controversial and failed policies of his second term damaged the reputation of the entire British government in India and stoked up the campaigns which would, within 50 years, see the British give up India completely.

Curzon had two clear objectives: first, to make India's territory less vulnerable to external threats and, second, to make British administration of India more efficient, more respected and therefore less vulnerable to criticism and political threats. In pursuit of both objectives, he embarked on reorganisation of certain provinces. The disastrous partition of the province of Bengal merits more detailed analysis further below.

Frontier policy

Curzon's greatest success was the creation of a buffer zone between the developed civilisation of the Indo-Gangetic plains and the lawless Afghan tribal areas – the 'wild north-west', so to speak. Beyond lay the Russian Empire with which Britain had engaged in **the Great Game** throughout the latter half of the nineteenth century.

Key term

The Great Game
The spying and skirmishing that accompanied the continuing Russo-British rivalry and competition.

In this volatile area, Curzon replaced British troops, whose presence was itself creating tension within the territory, with a new military force of local warriors under British command. Then, in 1901, he separated out from the Punjab a new North West Frontier Province to create more direct responsibility more likely to be respected by local warlords. This dangerous area, now straddling the border between Pakistan and Afghanistan, still remains out of the direct control of either government.

Key date

North West Frontier Province created: 1901

In Jammu and Kashmir province, control was extended further north to the mountainous edges of the Russian and Chinese Empires. This expansion too remains politically sensitive and was the cause of war between India and China in 1962.

Finally, and most spectacularly, Curzon became convinced that the Russians were moving into Tibet, an area beyond the Himalaya ruled by Buddhist monks and controlled by China. In 1904, Curzon ordered Sir Francis Younghusband to lead an expedition to investigate. They encountered no Russians and annexed Tibet but only by machine-gunning monks trying to defend their territory. The image of a civilised, competent British Empire was seriously tarnished.

Profile: Lord Curzon 1859–1925

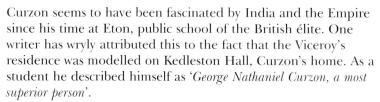

1859		– Born in Derbyshire
1885		– Entered Parliament
1887		– Extensive travels in Asia
1891–2		– Undersecretary for India
1895–8		– Undersecretary for Foreign Affairs
1899	January	– Viceroy of India
1905	November	– Resigned as Viceroy
1925		– Died

Curzon seems to have been fascinated by India and the Empire since his time at Eton, public school of the British élite. One writer has wryly attributed this to the fact that the Viceroy's residence was modelled on Kedleston Hall, Curzon's home. As a student he described himself as '*George Nathaniel Curzon, a most superior person*'.

Curzon was passionate about the value of India, politically and culturally. He saw the position of Viceroy as his destiny and, unprecedently, sought to be appointed. His letters to politicians demonstrate his conviction about the importance of India to the Empire: 'We have not the smallest intention of abandoning our Indian possessions and … it is highly improbable that any such intention will be entertained by our posterity.'

Curzon was high-minded and the scourge of British incompetence and injustice when he felt it threatened the moral and practical authority of the British minority in India. When the officers of the West Kent Regiment failed to investigate the gang rape of an elderly Burmese woman by their soldiers, Curzon had the entire regiment posted to the Arabian desert region of Aden for two years without leave.

However, his high self-regard led to his downfall in a political trial of strength between himself and the commander-in-chief of the Indian Army, Lord Kitchener. Curzon offered his resignation (as a tactic) and was astounded to find it accepted in the aftermath of the Bengal partition. His later career was disappointing. He did become Chancellor of Oxford University but, in 1912, he was still bitter enough to reject the suggestion of an honorary degree for the Indian poet Rabindranath Tagore, who would a year later receive the Nobel prize. There was perhaps tragic consolation in the ruin of Kitchener's reputation in the First World War.

Administrative policy

Curzon was a champion of both progress and conservation. He increased the railway network by 10,000 km (from 43,000 to 53,000 km) and the area of irrigated land by 3 million hectares. As well as a new department of agriculture, he established the Indian Archaeological Survey and worked to preserve architectural treasures, particularly the Taj Mahal.

Key question
How did Curzon try to improve India?

Within the British administration, Curzon's imperious manner also found a target in bureaucracy. He mocked the slowness of procedures and cut down reports and surveys. But he was not complacent. In 1904, he established a Criminal Investigation Department in every province with the aim of providing secret police reports on Indian political activities. Ironically, this led to criticism from some British governors of being too 'Russian'.

Curzon caused public controversy in his second term when he instituted an inquiry into the state of Indian higher education but failed to include any Indians on the inquiry committee. The resulting Universities Act (1904) aimed to restrict the huge growth in the number of private colleges and to include more centrally nominated officials on larger university governing bodies. The growing Indian middle class perceived an attack on its interest and an insult to its capability. Its resentment was ready to turn to resistance.

Curzon would shortly provide a perfect cause in the bungled partition of Bengal. First, however, we must catch up with political developments in the Congress Party.

Development of Congress to 1905

Key question
How did Congress move towards being a political party?

For many years after its foundation, Congress had remained what the name meant – a large meeting – which in its case was held every December in one of the Indian cities. Both Hindus and Muslims came to Congress and were prominent in its affairs. One early decision had been to ensure that its discussions did not alienate religious groups and weaken its claim to speak for all India.

The Congress had gained enormously in popularity among the educated and commercial middle class. The preparation for such a large conference was complex. It was not just the arrangement of accommodation for visitors from across the subcontinent but more importantly decisions about what, and what not, to discuss.

Over the years to the end of the nineteenth century, therefore, the organising committee became more important. The committee became the representatives of Congress and this created the conditions for a permanent political party. Congress debated its aims for India and the kind of demands it should make of the British government.

Of course, there were no general elections in which it might put up candidates. Congress adopted a strategy of lobbying MPs in Britain itself and so most of Congress' early activity was directed at raising money to fund a small organisation, office and newspaper in London.

Most of the demands of Congress were related to increasing education and access to positions in the administration of India. The British capital in India was Calcutta, in the populous province of Bengal, and so it was in Bengal that Indians saw most opportunity and experienced most disappointment. Bengal was home to a growing number of Indians who saw their situation in class terms. They were educated and ambitious but still squeezed out of the Indian Civil Service.

Partition of Bengal
Causes

Opinion is divided about the motivation for the plan to **partition** Bengal. On the one hand, the administration of Bengal had been recognised as a problem for a long time. Although a province in Indian terms, its population of 78 million people was twice as large as Britain's. Bengal was vulnerable to famine when the monsoon failed, but with such a concentration of workers it was also prone to unrest, such as the so-called Blue Mutiny of **indigo** workers.

In the period of the East India Company, when the Governor of the Presidency of Bengal was automatically also the Governor General of British India, a Lieutenant Governor for Bengal itself had been needed. In the late nineteenth century various plans had been discussed for reorganising the province to make it more manageable. Indeed, it was partly the endless deliberation about this matter which had provoked Curzon to streamline the bureaucracy and it was in Curzon's character to seek to resolve the problem itself in a robust way.

On the other hand, there were more immediate political motives. The success and confidence of Congress and the discontent among educated Bengalis disturbed the British. Curzon hinted at his aims by considering Congress' likely reaction when he wrote to the secretary of state in 1905 with the final partition proposal:

> Calcutta is the centre from which the Congress Party is manipulated throughout the whole of Bengal and indeed the whole of India … the whole of their activity is directed to creating an agency so powerful that they may one day be able to force a weak government to give them what they desire. Any measure in consequence that would divide the Bengali-speaking population; that would permit independent centres of activity and influence to grow up; that would dethrone Calcutta from its place as the centre of successful intrigue or that would weaken the lawyer class, who have the entire organisation in their hands, is intensely and hotly resented by them.

This is a classic expression of the policy of divide and rule. Indians were aware of these attitudes and nationalist historians have argued that this was the unspoken British policy behind territorial partition and creating divisions between Hindus or Congress and Muslims.

Partition

Despite a complete lack of formal consultation with Indians, Bengali or otherwise, the plan was approved by the secretary of state and came into effect on 16 October 1905.

Key question
Why did Curzon decide on partition?

Key terms

Partition
The formal division of a state or province.

Indigo
Purple dye from the the leaves of a plant.

Key date
Partition of Bengal: October 1905

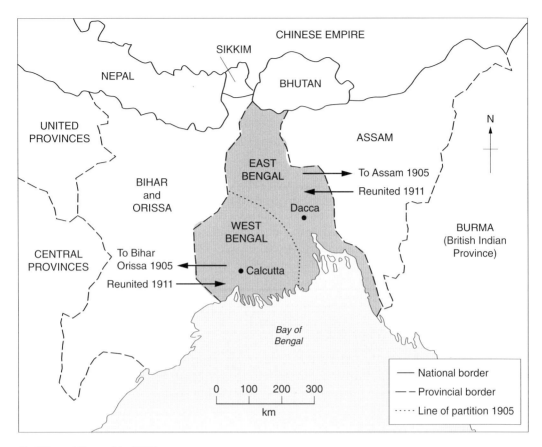

CHINESE EMPIRE

SIKKIM

NEPAL

BHUTAN

UNITED
PROVINCES

ASSAM

N

EAST
BENGAL

To Assam 1905

BIHAR
and
ORISSA

Reunited 1911

Dacca

WEST
BENGAL

BURMA
(British Indian
Province)

CENTRAL
PROVINCES

To Bihar
Orissa 1905

Calcutta

Reunited 1911

Bay of
Bengal

0   100   200   300

km

—— National border

— — Provincial border

· · · · · Line of partition 1905

Partition of Bengal in 1905.

Out of several adjacent provinces, two new provinces were
created:

- Western Bengal with Bihar and Orissa (and the provincial
  capital at Calcutta) had a total population of 54 million,
  including 42 million Hindus and nine million Muslims.
- Eastern Bengal with Assam (and the provincial capital at
  Dacca) had a total population of 31 million, including
  12 million Hindus and 18 million Muslims.

Reaction

The partition created a precedent for the reorganisation of
territory and government along religious lines.

The Bengali Hindus were outraged by what they saw as the
attempt to divide and rule. The partition cut right through the
unity of the Bengali-speaking community in order to create a
majority Muslim province with equal status. Not only that, within
Western Bengal itself, the Bengalis were outnumbered by the
populations of Bihar and Orissa.

In the short term, the Muslims were delighted with the majority
in the new eastern province. This would provide them with a
power base if and when Indians were able to elect provincial
governments.

Key question
What were the
political
consequences of
partition?

National protest

But it was more than a Bengali matter. Congress found itself at the head of a national unity of mood bringing together both the educated middle class and peasant-worker protesters while marginalising any lingering aristocratic leadership.

Three forms of protest action were adopted. In the first place, the normal channels of public discussion in newspaper articles and letters were of course used.

Swadesh

More significantly, there developed a popular campaign of **swadesh**. This was not a new idea and Indians could point to the non-cooperation campaign of the white British over the Ilbert Bill as a model. However, the Bengal *swadeshi* campaign seized the national imagination to create a feeling of self-respect. The *swadeshi* campaigns included a boycott of buying British goods and Lancashire cotton in particular, which was publicly burned. The anniversary of the partition was declared an annual day of mourning.

Key term

Swadesh
A campaign not to buy something – known as a boycott in English.

Terrorism

However, some were not satisfied with such passive resistance methods so there was also, thirdly, an increase in terrorist activity in Bengal. In 1908, two European women were killed when a bomb, intended for a local judge, was thrown into the wrong carriage. In 1909, the terrorism came to London, when an official at the India Office was shot in the street by a Punjabi seeking political martyrdom.

This caused a problem for Congress. There was a growing tension between those who believed in peaceful, lawful methods – the moderates – and those who wanted more urgent, direct, even violent action – the radicals or extremists. This tension would come to a head at the 1907 Congress in Surat.

Problems for the future

However, the first national unrest since the mutiny was if anything more of a problem for Curzon, whose second term of office ended under a cloud.

The radicals could credibly claim that the British would never be fair to Indians and even Gokhale, leader of the moderates, complained about the lack of consultation over the partition of Bengal. There was little evidence with which to resist demands for Congress to work towards independence from Britain.

On the other hand, the anger at the deliberate creation of a Muslim majority province suggested to Muslims that an independent India dominated politically by Hindu Congress would never be fair to their community.

From 1906, the new Liberal government was quietly determined to put things right without giving in straightaway.

Key date

Liberal government: December 1905

Key question
How did the moderates defeat the extremists?

Key terms

Resolution
A formal decision at a meeting, often voted on.

Swaraj
Literally self-rule, thus meaning independence.

Key date

Congress split at Surat: 1907

The Congress split

Congresses were held in the cool dry weather of December. Since the beginning, the efforts of the local Congress supporters (the reception committee) in the city where the Congress was to be held were rewarded with the honour of choosing the president to run the Congress.

The 1906 Congress was held in Calcutta, at the heart of Bengali protest, and seemed likely to swing in a radical direction. Strong efforts by the moderates succeeded in getting an ageing president elected for a third time as a compromise. They also managed to tone down various radical **resolutions**, including one in favour of *swaraj*, which was reinterpreted as meaning achievement of the same system of government as in the self-governing British colonies.

After the Congress, Gokhale toured the country promoting the moderate view of progress towards self-government within Empire and presenting *swadesh* as more like a positive choice of Indian goods rather than a boycott or rejection of British goods and institutions.

It became apparent that the radicals would make a redoubled attempt at the next Congress to prevent Congress leadership watering down their demands again.

The 1907 Congress was scheduled for Nagpur, a Maratha city and sympathetic to Tilak's radicals. At the last moment, the moderates switched the venue to Surat, one of their strongholds, which would ensure the president was one of them. Their final tactic was a proposal to change the constitution of Congress so that members would be obliged to accept the objective of self-government within the British Empire. In other words, it would be impossible to be a member of Congress and support radical demands. The moderates wanted no more debate on the subject and preferred simply to change the rules.

The heated proceedings were reported in the (Manchester) *Guardian* newspaper. After the election of a moderate president, there was an outburst of cries of 'Remember Nagpur!' and proceedings were suspended. When they resumed, Tilak asked to speak, was ignored and promptly started to interrupt the president's opening speech. There was even greater uproar, during which Gokhale attempted to physically protect his great rival. At some point, a shoe was thrown, a Maratha shoe of red leather with a sole made of lead, which struck one of the leaders. A full-scale brawl of hundreds broke out, the police arrived and proceedings were aborted.

It seemed to the radicals that the Congress had broken up. But the moderates met in private the next day, called a meeting which they termed a national convention and elected a convention committee which in due course framed a new Congress constitution requiring acceptance of the moderate objective of self-government within Empire.

It seemed to the moderates that they had succeeded. Indeed, for a decade the radicals were excluded from Congress. The moderate victory seemed complete when some of the radical

Profile: Gopal Krishna Gokhale 1866–1915

1866   – Born in Kolhat, western India
1886   – Schoolteacher after studying law
1889   – Member of Congress
1890   – Secretary to Poona Sarvajanik *Sabha*
1895   – Secretary of Congress
1897–1914   – Made several political visits to England
1902   – Elected to Imperial Legislative Council
1905–15   – President of Congress
1915   – Died

Gokhale was born into a Brahmin family from western India. He was drawn to mainstream Indian nationalism and rose rapidly through a series of political appointments.

Gokhale was an admirer of the British Raj, seeing it as an opportunity to prepare India for self-government on a secular basis. He favoured cooperation with the British and persuasion with Indians. He wanted self-government but it had to be achieved through constructive political means, supported by social reform, especially more and better education. He opposed mass action, especially anything which challenged authority or law and order.

Nevertheless, Gokhale was a devastating critic of the British within the political arena. He used an annual opportunity to discuss the budget in the Imperial Legislative Council to survey the entire rule of the British in India.

Gokhale appealed to the cautious Indian middle class and was in tune with the British Liberal government, working closely with John Morley, Secretary of State for India. His leadership of Congress ensured that the moderate view prevailed.

Gandhi recognised Gokhale as an admirable leader and master politician, describing him as 'pure as crystal, gentle as a lamb, brave as a lion and chivalrous to a fault and the most perfect man in the political field'.

leaders, including Tilak, were convicted of incitement to terrorism and deported to the Burmese territories. However, it soon became clear that this was a hollow victory, cutting Congress off from the public mood.

Muslim political developments

Political development in the Muslim community was muted, being more focused on the educational and social activities of the Aligarh movement.

In 1906, two modest, but significant events began the growth of a political force which would eventually demand and achieve a separate Muslim state.

Profile: Bal Gangadhar Tilak 1856–1920

1856 – Born in Ratnagiri, western India
1876 – Studied law
1881 – Editor of the Kesari and Mahratta political journals
1884 – Formed Deccan Education Society (DES)
1890 – Resigned from the DES
1896 – Started the Shivaji festival
1897 – Convicted of sedition, sentenced to 18 months' hard labour
1908 – Deported to Burma for six years
1920 – Died

Tilak, like Gokhale, was born into a Brahmin family from western India and drawn to journalism and politics by the opportunities for passionate protest.

Tilak was inspired by the glorious, rebellious Marathas and created new festivals to celebrate Hindu leaders of the past, especially Shivaji. He regarded the British Raj as something to be ejected from India. He objected to Christian missionary work and took a conservative Hindu approach to social reform. He worked hard on local projects to increase Indian education but always considered political objectives more important than social reforms.

Tilak appealed to the uneducated masses and favoured direct action and boycotts. He took support from the Japanese (i.e. Asian) victory over the Russian (i.e. European) Empire in 1905.

Tilak was a forceful character and provocative. He emphasised rights over concessions and made demands not requests. In 1906 he said:

Key date

Russia defeated by Japan: 1905

> If you forget your grievances by hearing words of sympathy, then the cause is gone. You must make a permanent cause of grievance. Store up the grievances till they are removed. Partition [of Bengal] grievance will be the edifice for the regeneration of India.

After his deportation to Burma, however, Tilak was a changed man. He rejected violent methods and Hindu victories. He helped bring about the Lucknow Pact between Congress and the Muslim League and supported the Khilafat movement.

Tilak's extremist movement had been shut out of Congress by Gokhale, but its methods and ambitions lived on in the campaigns of Gandhi.

The Simla delegation

The fury of Hindus over the creation of a Muslim-majority province in the partition of Bengal had convinced Muslims that, as and when Indians were permitted to take part in government, they would be overwhelmed by the general Hindu majority.

Following Curzon's ignominious departure, the new viceroy, Lord Minto, and a British Liberal government had indicated that reforms would be considered.

A delegation of some 70 Muslim leaders travelled to the British summer capital of Simla in October 1906 to present their plan for separate electorates for Muslims in any future political reforms. Lord Minto responded very sympathetically to the demand, seen by some historians as trying to encourage a loyal Muslim political strength to counterbalance the growth of Congress.

Simla delegation:
October 1906

All-India Muslim
League formed: 1906

Key dates

The All-India Muslim League

Cheered by Minto's sympathetic response, the leader of the Simla delegation, the Aga Khan, urged the creation of a Muslim political organisation to keep up the momentum of the campaign.

As a result, in December 1906, the All-India Muslim League was founded at Dacca, Bengal (later Dhaka, capital of Bangladesh) by Nawab Viqar-ul-Mulq. It was for many years little more than a debating society for its educated, middle-class members. By 1916, however, it was sufficiently important to be part of the agreement with Congress over future political demands known as the Lucknow Pact (see page 47).

The Morley–Minto reforms
Motives

The new Liberal government in Britain took its responsibility for India seriously, but interpreted the duty of care in a less paternalistic and more trusting manner. The perception was that the gulf between the rulers and the ruled had widened and this was not only bad in itself but politically negligent. The government had been caught out by the sudden and widespread agitation over the partition of Bengal and the support for *swadesh*. The fear of mutiny lurked behind the sense of being out of touch. The number of police informers was increased.

Key question
How did the Liberal
government try to
improve Indian
government?

In 1908, the government established a Royal Commission on Decentralisation to recommend improvements to the administration of India. Politically and strategically, the wish was to increase the contact with public opinion into the administration. The commission's report recommended modest increases in the numbers of Indians on the various legislative councils which formed the hierarchy of Indian administration.

The recommendations were championed by the secretary of state in Britain, John Morley, and the viceroy in India, Lord Minto, whose names supply the popular title for the resulting reforms.

The Indian moderates had high hopes of Morley, who had been a firm supporter of Gladstone's plans for home rule, that is self-government, in Ireland in the 1880s. Now 68 years old, Morley was keen to leave a mark on political history. However, he informed Gokhale, during the latter's visit to Britain, that reform would not lead to an Indian Parliament or self-government in the foreseeable future. The reforms were intended to produce better informed and more effective government by the British.

In addition, Morley and Minto made it clear to the moderates that, while it was fully expected that the radicals would be scornful of the modest scale of the change, if the moderates expressed disappointment then the whole project would be dropped.

The 1909 Indian Councils Act

Key date

Indian Councils Act: 1909

The Morley–Minto reforms became law in the Indian Councils Act 1909.

There were modest changes to the following legislative councils:

- provincial
- central
- executive.

Most councils retained a majority of officials rather than elected members. Moreover, the Indian members were to be elected indirectly. That is, various organisations and social groups were permitted to choose a specified number of representatives who were recommended to the council in question. These recommendations were never rejected, but neither was there a principle of direct candidature and election to the councils in a parliamentary style. The constituencies were very small, in some cases as few as 20 people. The total number of votes was just 4000. The total elected membership of all the councils was 135 (up from the 39 permitted in the 1892 Indian Councils Act).

The consequences

Key question
Did the reforms satisfy Indians?

The regulations determining the respective organisations and groups eligible to elect representatives were published a while after the act. Now Congress, which had publicly supported the reforms, protested while the Muslims, who had initially complained, were satisfied.

This was because, for the first time, council seats were reserved distinctively for Muslims, among several other social groups such as universities. The stated purpose of the reform was to bring in a cross-section of public opinion and this could only be guaranteed by reserving numbers of seats for specified groups. It was, however, a crucial precedent for all the constitutional reform to follow including national partition at independence. There would be no going back.

The councils remained advisory. They could initiate debates (with certain subjects prohibited) and comment on proposals but all their resulting recommendations could be ignored by the executive. Some seized the opportunity: Gokhale used the annual debate on the Indian budget to make wide-ranging speeches about the state of Indian affairs. The Muslims participated whole-heartedly and Muhammad Ali Jinnah, the future leader of Pakistan, became an elected representative with some optimism for a while.

In due course, however, the different defects of the measures became apparent. For the Indians, it became clear that nothing much had changed however well-intentioned the reform. By 1917, of the 168 resolutions made in the imperial legislative council, 76 were rejected by the government, 68 were withdrawn and just 24 were accepted.

For the British, it became clear that their own retention of control of councils (through a majority of unelected officials) placed the elected Indian members in the position of being able to complain all the time without having to do anything about the matters in question. The Indian groups became, in the words of one historian, the **official opposition** to the British government. In the view of the former Viceroy Curzon, the increase in Indian intervention actually reduced the sense of care in the British élite.

> **Official opposition** The largest minority group in a parliament.
>
> *Key term*

Bengal and Delhi

Having granted Muslims separate electorates, the British felt able to balance this with the reunification of Bengal. The partition had created a Muslim-majority province. In 1911, the boundaries were revised so that Assam and Bihar-and-Orissa became separate provinces while Bengal itself was reunited. This placated Hindus, but profoundly disappointed Muslims, although they were pleased at the simultaneous transfer of the capital of British India from Calcutta, the East India Company city, to Delhi, the historic Mughal capital.

> Bengal reunited, Delhi became British capital: 1911
>
> *Key date*

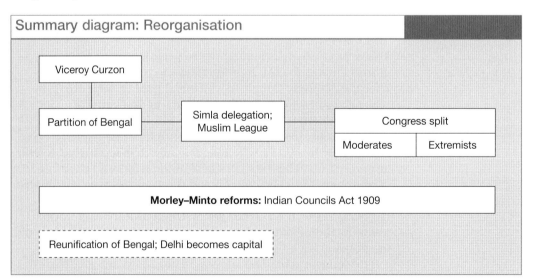

Summary diagram: Reorganisation

- Viceroy Curzon
- Partition of Bengal
- Simla delegation; Muslim League
- Congress split
  - Moderates
  - Extremists
- **Morley–Minto reforms:** Indian Councils Act 1909
- Reunification of Bengal; Delhi becomes capital

2 | Reconciliation in Conflict

The Great War

For the most part, the Indian population supported Britain in the war. Thousands of individuals volunteered for military service and politicians pledged their loyalty. But it was clear that Britain would need to reward this support and sacrifice with

> Outbreak of the Great War (later called the First World War): 1914
>
> *Key date*

constitutional progress. Within months of the start of the war, Prime Minister Lord Asquith conceded that:

> henceforth Indian questions would have to be approached from a new angle of vision.

In a short space of time, Indian public opinion also gained a new perspective on the British Empire and Europeans in general. This was partly the result of distant observation of the strategic situation and partly the result of reports of individual experiences.

Key question
How did the war change Indian views of Britain?

The strategic situation

In the first place, it became apparent that Britain was no longer the supreme global empire. Although not fighting for its existence, it was certainly contesting with equally powerful forces and was not invincible. Britain's alliance with Russia (and France) meant that a wartime threat to India from the north was inconceivable. However, in the event of Britain's defeat, then Russia might march in. This concentrated Indian minds on supporting the British war effort.

On the other hand, even in the event of victory, the war would be likely to have weakened Britain's power, creating much more favourable conditions for the nationalist movement.

It was, of course, not immediately obvious that the war would be a world war (nor indeed just the first). It involved nations with global empires but the predominant theatre of war was Europe and the Western Front across Belgium and France in particular. Accordingly, Indian regiments were transported to Europe and then fought in the horrifying conditions of the trenches. The effect of their experiences on Indian public opinion was significant.

Military experiences

The moral high ground of the white man's burden turned into the blood-soaked swamp of trench warfare. To the Indians, the carnage of the Great War proved that the Europeans were no better and perhaps worse than those they ruled. Indeed, the fighting between white European neighbours (and the family kinship of the Kaiser, the Tsar and the King-Emperor of Britain) could be described in the same terms as 'communal' fighting between Indian Hindus and Muslims.

This observation of European barbarity was aggravated by the sheer incompetence of the major campaign in which Indian troops were involved: **Mesopotamia**. The troops were shockingly under-equipped and badly led. Indian industry was not geared to production of weapons or vehicles and the British could not afford to divert supplies from the European war. The campaign limped on and acquired the nickname the 'Mess-Pot'. Thousands of Indian troops were forced to surrender in the siege of Kut, but eventually the British forces prevailed with the capture of Baghdad.

Key term

Mesopotamia
The Middle East, especially now Iraq, from the Greek for 'between rivers' (the Tigris and Euphrates in Iraq).

Agitation

The opening of hostilities had also seen the open expression of loyalty to the British Empire from politicians and the people. The British declared at first that all hopes and plans for further nationalist progress should be set aside for as long as the war lasted. However, although support remained strong, there were reminders that political goals had not been forgotten. Indeed, the war presented new opportunities.

Key question
How did political protest re-emerge?

The *Ghadr* movement

Most disturbing for the British were a number of mutinies. There were two early mutinies of Pathans in the winter of 1914–15 apparently caused by fear that they would be led by Muslim officers. Indian troops in Singapore had learned from reports and personal letters about the death toll at the Battle of the Somme (1916). A rumour that they were to embark for France led to a rampage and the killing of European civilians, including women. One woman wrote later that they thought the horrors of the mutiny were about to be repeated. In fact, order was quickly established and 37 ringleaders were publicly executed.

The most politically significant mutiny never actually took place. In early 1914, a Japanese steamer, the *Komagata Maru*, was commissioned by more than 300 Sikhs working in Malaya to take them to Canada. The Canadians refused entry despite the voyage complying with new anti-Asian immigration laws. After months in harbour, the *Komagata Maru* set sail for Calcutta.

By the time it arrived, in September 1914, war had broken out and suspicions were high. It was known that the Canadian coastal province of British Columbia was home to a growing community of anti-British Indians. The movement gave its name – ***Ghadr*** – to a newspaper widely distributed in North America and the East which had the sub-title 'enemy of the British government'.

The Sikhs found troops waiting to escort them to a holding camp. Some made a break for the city and 22 were shot. The rest were rounded up and transported across India. The incident inflamed anti-British feeling in the Punjab, still more so when an official inquiry blamed the immigrant Sikhs.

Subsequently, British secret police paid close attention to politics in the Punjab. Inside information led to the break-up of a planned uprising in 1915. Five thousand Ghadrites were arrested, 200 jailed or transported abroad and 46 were hanged. The relief and satisfaction of the British was haunted by the realisation that the traditional loyalty of the Punjab (compared with the continuous agitation of Bengal) could no longer be counted on. Just four years later, this anxiety would lead to the worst atrocity of British rule in India.

Ghadr
Translates as mutiny.

Key term

Home rule leagues
Origins

Key date

Formation of home rule leagues: 1916

In 1916 two new political organisations were launched. Both had the aim of campaigning for home rule for India. One was led by the ejected Congress radical Tilak (see page 39); the other by a forceful 69-year-old British woman called Mrs Annie Besant.

The home rule leagues were based closely on the campaigns for home rule in Ireland in the late nineteenth century. An Irish parliamentary party had been formed to work democratically for self-government in Ireland while remaining part of the British Empire. It took four attempts between 1886 and 1914 for an Irish Home Rule Bill to become law and even then it was suspended because of the outbreak of war. However, its ultimate implementation was inevitable.

In the Indian context, this struggle showed that home rule was a challenging but realistic objective. It could not be dismissed as too easy. Although Congress had discussed home rule since 1905, the control of the moderates had ensured that it never became a campaign. But Congress had lost momentum and influence since the 1907 split. Besant tried at first to work with Congress and revive its fortunes, but she soon realised that Congress was only interested in controlling and suppressing the home rule movement.

Key question

Why did home rule leagues have appeal?

Home rule

Home rule was not revolutionary. Indeed the term was adopted, in the opinion of one nationalist, N.C. Kelkar, because it was:

> familiar to the English ear and saved them from all the imaginary terrors which the word *swaraj* was likely to conjure up in their minds.

Home rule would involve only management of internal Indian affairs. Defence and foreign policy would remain matters for the British government. Besant stated that it meant 'freedom without separation'; Tilak emphasised that it sought 'reform of the system of administration and not the overthrow of government'. In a more religious comparison, he spoke of the Indian people maintaining faith in the divine Emperor while seeking a new set of priests.

Above all, the First World War moderated attitudes. There was an overriding loyalty to the British even though patriotic pride in the Indian contribution to the war effort simultaneously boosted nationalism. Tilak himself stated in 1917:

> If you want Home Rule be prepared to defend your Home … You cannot reasonably say that the ruling will be done by you and the fighting for you.

Success

Tilak's Home Rule League for India rapidly gained 32,000 members despite being focused on just the two regions of Maharashtra and Karnataka. Besant's All-India Home Rule League was smaller and grew more slowly but its network of committees covered most of the rest of India. The two were mutually supportive: Tilak and Besant joined each other's organisations. They toured the country giving public lectures and publishing pamphlets. They successfully generated agitation amongst the public in a way that Congress had never really tried.

Responses

Congress maintained its moderate reluctance to demand something as radical as home rule even though people joined home rule leagues in great numbers (including two future national leaders, Nehru and Jinnah). Other Indian groups were also resistant, especially Muslims and lower-caste Hindu groups who thought self-government would entrench Brahmin Hindu dominance. They viewed the British as more protective of their interests.

The British regarded the home rule leagues with great concern. They had finally calmed the agitation caused by the partition of Bengal by reuniting it in 1911 and liked the tame approach of the moderate-controlled Congress. One official reported:

> Moderate leaders can command no support among the vocal classes who are being led at the heels of Tilak and Besant.

Orders were given for swift arrest of home rule campaigners whenever possible. Students were forbidden from holding meetings at which home rule might be discussed. Tilak was arrested on charges of sedition and required to put up 40,000 **rupees** as **surety** of good behaviour. Besant was actually **interned**.

These moves were completely counter-productive. Congress moderates now swung their support over to home rule campaigns. The viceroy wrote to the secretary of state:

> Mrs Besant, Tilak and the others are fomenting with great vigour the agitation for immediate home rule and in the absence of any definite announcement by the government of India as to their policy in the matter, it is attracting many of those who hitherto have held less advanced views.

Consequences

The British government realised the need to respond at least with words if not actions. On 20 August 1917, it issued a declaration which appeared to promise eventual self-government. The declaration, known in British historiography as the Montagu Declaration after the secretary of state who made it, had the desired effect of taking the wind out of the home rule sails without making definite commitments.

When Besant was freed, she was triumphantly elected President of Congress in December 1917. There were great hopes for the reunification and revival of Congress. However, she proved an inconsistent and ineffective leader of Congress. She was crucially

Key terms

Rupee
The currency of India.

Surety
A deposit lost in the event of breaking the law.

Interned
Imprisoned without trial.

Key question
Why did home rule leagues fail?

Key date

The Montagu Declaration: 20 August 1917

reluctant to support any kind of boycott or resistance campaigns. Tilak still refrained from rejoining Congress.

The home rule movement quickly lost momentum and, strictly speaking, it failed to achieve its objectives. However, it had created the first truly national mass campaign. Moreover, its failure actually left an unsatisfied willingness among the general population for more direct action. This is widely believed to have prepared the way for the campaigns of Gandhi from the 1920s onwards.

The Lucknow Pact

Key date

Lucknow Pact: December 1916

Key term

Pact
An agreement between political allies.

At the Congress meeting of December 1916 in Lucknow, a historic agreement was reached between the predominantly Hindu Congress and the All-India Muslim League. The so-called Lucknow **Pact** covered not only a broad statement of political objective but also the precise details of future electorates, once India was self-governing. The sense of occasion was further enhanced by the re-integration of the radical wing of the Congress Party at the same session.

On the Congress side, President A.C. Mazumdar reflected on:

nearly ten years of painful separation and wandering through the wilderness of misunderstandings and the mazes of unpleasant controversies … There are occasional differences even in the best regulated families.

On the Muslim side, there was resentment against the British over:

- the 1911 reversal of the partition of Bengal which had originally been of benefit to Muslim politicians; and
- the declaration of war against Turkey, home of the Ottoman Sultan, the head of the international Muslim community.

In 1915, Congress and the Muslim League had held concurrent sessions in Bombay and both had declared self-government as their political objective. During 1916, two committees had worked together to prepare the details of a scheme for how such self-government would work. Concurrent sessions were held again in Lucknow and the scheme was accepted by the two political groups. It was not, of course, in their power to bring it about.

Table 2.1: Muslim proportions of provincial populations and planned seats in provincial councils as part of Lucknow Pact

Province	Muslim population (%)	Planned seats (%)
Punjab	Over 50	50
Bengal	Over 50	40
United Provinces	14	30
Bihar	13	25
Central Provinces	4	} 15
Madras	7	
Bombay	20	33.3

The heart of the scheme was the set of proportions of seats in the provincial legislative councils reserved for Muslims (Table 2.1). This took forward the precedent created by the Morley–Minto reforms of separate communal elections for quotas of seats in the councils. What was remarkable was the extent to which Congress agreed to weighting the representation above the proportion of the actual population in many provinces.

Further communal agreements in the plan included:

- No Muslim would contest a seat outside the reserved quota.
- No bill or clause would proceed if 75 per cent of the affected community opposed it.
- The central Legislative Council would increase to 150 members of whom 80 per cent would be elected and one-third of them would be Muslim in the proportions set out for the provinces, thus giving Muslims additional weightage at both provincial and central levels.

There were more general agreements such as:

- Provincial councillors would serve for five years.
- Councils would have powers over revenue collection, loans and expenditure.
- Indians would form at least half the members of the Executive Council.
- The judiciary would be independent of the executive, the government of India independent of the secretary of state, and the India Council in Britain would be abolished.
- Defence, foreign affairs and diplomacy would remain British responsibilities.

The Muslim League leader Jinnah stated that 'cooperation in the cause of the motherland should be our guiding principle'. To the British, it did indeed seem that the nationalist movement was reuniting and gaining strength.

The Montagu declaration

By 1917, it was clear to the British that there was no benefit in postponing political concessions until after the war.

Key question
How did the British respond to Indian unity?

Accordingly, Edwin Montagu, secretary of state for India, announced a startling new constitutional objective in the House of Commons on 20 August:

> The increasing association of Indians in every branch of the administration and the gradual development of self-governing institutions with a view to the progressive realisation of responsible government in India as part of the British Empire.

The first part of the declaration was no more than a restatement of the Proclamation of Victoria some 50 years earlier. Moreover, the language of 'with a view to the progressive realisation' and 'as part of the British Empire', carried echoes of hoping this would all take a long time. However, the promise of 'self-governing institutions' was a clear and significant concession that an Indian parliament, controlling the Indian administration, would be created.

Montagu promptly set off on a massive tour of India to consult politicians and public opinion. His findings were published in the 1918 Montagu–Chelmsford report which would become the basis for the 1919 legislation.

However, by the time the reforms became law, events at Amritsar in the Punjab would have sealed the fate of the British Empire in India.

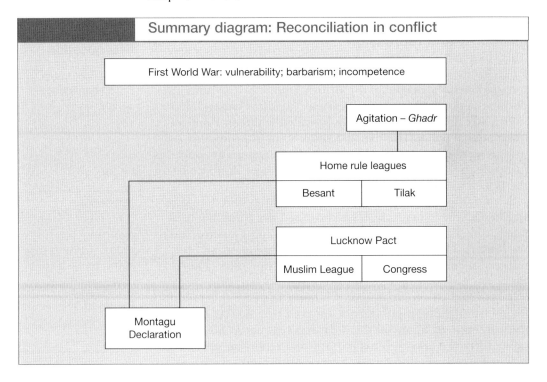

Summary diagram: Reconciliation in conflict

3 | The Amritsar Massacre

Political consequences of the First World War

The British had been drawn into the Mesopotamian campaign by French and Russian desires to break up the Ottoman Empire. There was great British reluctance to go to war against this Islamic empire because of the possible reaction within India in particular.

It was hoped in India, among the British élite as much as the Indian population, that the Mesopotamian region would become a British-controlled buffer zone to protect the western approach to India. However, further political factors came into play. Irregular Arab forces (some led by Lawrence of Arabia) had scored minor, but spectacular successes against Ottoman Turkish forces and supply lines. The British had promised them some form of independence once the Ottoman Empire was broken up. One such consequence was the creation of an Arab state of Iraq. The British in India were dismayed by this whole-hearted support for nationalist demands. How could similar demands within India be denied?

As a recognition of its sacrifice, but also perhaps in the new mood of nation-building, India was permitted its own representatives at the Imperial War Conference of 1917. This gave it a status comparable to the self-governing Dominions of the British Empire. The conference was called to discuss the shape of the eventual political settlement after the expected victory of the Allied powers. When victory was finally achieved, India also took part in the formal peace-treaty negotiations.

Insecurity and repression

The Allies had won the war, but the British felt far from secure. First, the arrival of US forces on the Western Front from 1917 foreshadowed the eclipse of the British Empire by the Americans during the twentieth century. President Woodrow Wilson felt sufficiently supreme to declare his so-called Fourteen Points of international policy. These included the right of peoples to independent nationhood. The constant US pressure to apply this principle to the British Empire would have major significance for the British in India.

Second, the Russian Revolution in 1917 had resulted in a **Bolshevik** government which had executed the entire imperial family (the Tsar being cousin of the British King-Emperor and the Kaiser). They had also withdrawn from the war as an imperialist conflict nearly causing defeat for the Allies. The European powers feared the spread of Bolshevism. British soldiers who had expected to return home in peacetime found themselves fighting inside Russia against a new Red Army in the vain hope of killing off the Bolshevik regime. At home, the police formed a Special Branch to spy and report on suspicious political activity. In due course, Special Branch officers in Britain and India would be reporting on Indian independence campaigners.

Finally, the world was devastated by a flu **pandemic** which took more lives in the winter of 1918–19 than the four years of the war.

The Rowlatt Act

In this insecure state of affairs the British were not inclined to relax their guard in India, despite or perhaps because of the commitment given in the Montagu declaration. The British government in India had passed the Defence of India Act (1915) permitting them to close down newspapers suspected of anti-British attitudes for the duration of the war.

Indians had expected that with the end of the war these laws would become inactive, if not explicitly repealed. In fact, the British quickly moved to renew their powers by passing the Anarchical and Revolutionary Crimes Act (1919), now more commonly termed the Rowlatt Act, after its creator.

Key question
Why did the end of the war not boost British confidence?

Key terms

Bolshevik
A member of the majority, thus the political group that emerged as leader of the revolution.

Pandemic
Global epidemic.

Key dates

End of the First World War: 1918

US President Wilson's Fourteen Points: 1918

Rowlatt Act: 1919

Key question
How did the British maintain suppression?

The Act enabled the powers of the Defence of India Act to be invoked if it was judged anarchic conditions were developing. These powers included unlimited detention without trial, trial without jury and the use of evidence illegal in peacetime. A wide range of activities constituted anarchic behaviour. For example, it was now an offence punishable by two years' imprisonment to possess a copy of a **seditious** newspaper.

All 22 Indian members of the Imperial Legislative Council had opposed the bill, but the majority of appointed officials ensured that it was passed.

Jinnah resigned from the Council stating that the Act 'ruthlessly trampled upon the principles for which Great Britain avowedly fought the war'. Gandhi declared it a betrayal of wartime support by Indians and declared a national *hartal* on 6 April 1919, which was widely supported and reinforced the alarming unity of Hindu and Muslim campaigners. The *hartal* turned to widespread violence, not least in the cities of the Punjab, unleashing the terrible events at Amritsar in 1919.

The Bengali poet Rabindranath Tagore would later describe the Amritsar Massacre as 'the monstrous progeny of a monstrous war'.

Key terms

Seditious
Encouraging overthrow of a government.

Hartal
Strike action, refusal to work.

An artist's impression of the Amritsar Massacre. What weapons are shown? To what extent are the Indians presented as a threat?

The Amritsar Massacre

Amritsar is the holy city of the Sikhs at the centre of the Punjab. Punjabis had played a major role in the war, but also in the *Ghadr* movement. There was a strong mood of resentment at the continued repression in the form of the Rowlatt Act. On the British side, there was a renewed fear of uprising and mutiny.

The Jallianwala Bagh meeting

Congress declared another *hartal* for 8 April which was widely supported, but led to violent attacks on people and buildings. On 10 April a mob killed five Englishmen and left an Englishwoman for dead. The Punjab provincial government requested military assistance and control.

Troops under the command of General Dyer arrived in Amritsar on the evening of 11 April. Dyer banned all public meetings and arrested local politicians. Dyer was determined not to repeat the accepted error of the 1857 mutiny by letting events get out of control. As he explained later, he was even more determined to teach the Punjabis a lesson.

However, the ban was defied by the call for a public meeting on 13 April in the Jallianwala Bagh. This was an open space within the town that had originally been a set of gardens, but was now enclosed on all sides by the backs of buildings and a high wall. Between 10,000 and 20,000 Punjabis were crammed into the garden when Dyer arrived with Indian troops. He also had an armoured car with a machine gun on top. It is a small mercy that this was unable to enter the garden because the alleyway was too small.

Key date
Amritsar Massacre: 13 April 1919

Dyer's troops ran in, took up line position and, without warning, started firing into the crowd. There were only three or four other, very narrow, exits. Panic ensued and people were crushed together. Dyer interpreted this as the gathering of a charge and directed fire into the thickest groups. His troops used over 1600 bullets and only stopped firing because the ammunition ran out. Dyer later confirmed that had there been more ammunition he would have continued the onslaught. It is accepted that 379 people were killed within minutes. The 1200 wounded were left to fend for themselves.

In the days that followed, Dyer imposed **martial law** and humiliating punishments that drew international criticism. Public floggings were held of Indians suspected, but not convicted, of violence. In the street where an Englishwoman had been attacked, Indians were forced to crawl along the ground.

Key term
Martial law
Army imposes its own rules, suspends civil courts and justice.

The Hunter Inquiry

British and worldwide concern eventually forced the government to hold an inquiry. In various statements to the Hunter Inquiry committee and elsewhere, Dyer made it abundantly clear that:

Key question
How did Dyer justify himself?

It was no longer a question of merely dispersing the crowd but one of producing a sufficient moral effect, from a military point of view, not only on those who were present, but more especially

throughout the Panjab. There could be no question of undue
severity.

Dyer maintained that the situation was on the verge of complete
mob challenge to the British authority in India and a threat to
the lives of Europeans. In this view, he was clearly supported by
British public opinion, to the lasting disgust of Indians. The
House of Lords passed a vote of thanks for his actions and a
public subscription raised thousands of pounds in reward.

The inquiry committee was split along ethnic lines. The
majority report held Dyer responsible but only **censured** him.
The minority report of the three Indian members of the inquiry
blamed martial law for the agitation and compared Dyer's actions
to the brutality of the Germans during the war.

Even to the majority, it was inexcusable that Dyer did not
attempt to prevent the meeting coming together and that he
agreed that he could have dispersed the crowd without firing but
would have 'looked a fool'.

Dyer's weak excuses, on top of his declared aim of terrorising
the entire Punjab, have led some nationalist writers to claim that
the massacre was planned. There is no evidence of this, but if true
it was certainly a terrible misjudgement. For the moral authority

Key term

Censure
A formal political
reprimand.

Key question
Why did the Amritsar
Massacre weaken the
British?

Contemporary
cartoon after Amritsar.
How is British
authority
characterised? How
does the action of the
colonial victims recall
punishments after the
Amritsar Massacre?

of the British was forever broken. Never again could the British claim to be ruling India with the aim of developing civilised public values or even that they governed by the rule of law.

Gandhi declared that: 'cooperation in any shape or form with this satanic government is sinful'. The freedom struggle was reinvigorated. Dyer believed his actions to have been decisive. They were. In the words of a later historian, Amritsar was the massacre which destroyed the Raj.

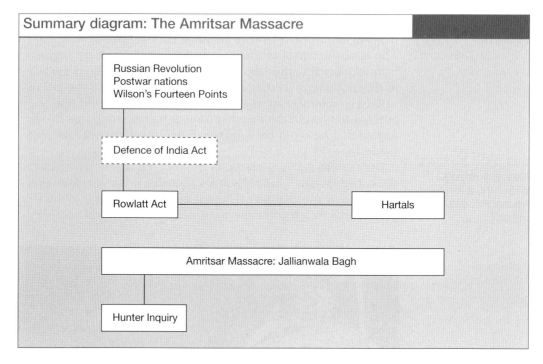

Summary diagram: The Amritsar Massacre

- Russian Revolution
- Postwar nations
- Wilson's Fourteen Points
- Defence of India Act
- Rowlatt Act — Hartals
- Amritsar Massacre: Jallianwala Bagh
- Hunter Inquiry

4 | The Montagu–Chelmsford Reforms

Government of India Act 1919

In December 1919, the Government of India Act was passed. As this was based on the Montagu–Chelmsford Report of 1918, it was more commonly known as the Montagu–Chelmsford reforms (or even Mont–ford reforms). The provisions of the Act were inaugurated in 1921.

In the British view, this showed that the government was clearly following through the promise of the 1917 Montagu Declaration. To Indians, however, the four years from declaration to implementation contrasted significantly with the weeks taken to pass the repressive Rowlatt Act. Moreover, coming just eight months after the Amritsar Massacre, there was little feeling of success let alone gratitude.

The Act contained three significant features:

- self-government in the future
- changes to the composition of councils and the electorate
- division of governmental responsibilities.

Key question
What did the Government of India Act change?

Government of India Act: December 1919

Key date

Self-government

The Act confirmed the promise of eventual self-government of India by an Indian Parliament. It promised a review in ten years time of the success of the actual changes in the Act. Then a decision about the next move to dominion status might be taken. It made no reference to independence from Britain at any time.

Councils and electorates

The most significant feature in this area was the elimination of the majorities of appointed officials in most legislative councils. For the first time, members elected by Indians would be in the majority.

At the very top, the Imperial Executive Council was increased to six members, plus the viceroy and the commander-in-chief, of whom three would be (appointed) Indians.

The two houses of the central legislature comprised the (lower) legislative assembly in which 106 members would be elected and 40 nominated, and the (higher) council of state would have 61 members (elected by the wealthiest individuals).

The provincial legislative councils were expanded so that 70% of members were elected. All provinces now had full governors and executive councils.

With regard to the electorate, the national **franchise** was extended according to levels of property tax, in other words, wealth of males. Out of a population of some 150 million people, five million were able to vote for provincial councils, one million for the Legislative Assembly and just 17,000 for the Council of State.

Furthermore, the principle of separate candidates and electorates was firmly embedded. As well as general electorates, in which all those enfranchised could vote, there were 'reserved' elections of Muslim, Sikh and Christian members by their own electorates (subject still to the property qualification). There were also special electorates for universities (as in Britain until 1950), landholders and business interests.

Dyarchy

The new division of responsibilities within the administration of India took place at two levels – **dyarchy**. In the first place, responsibility for a number of matters was transferred from the central Indian government to provincial administrations. The provinces became responsible for collecting land tax, **excise** duty and revenue from stamps. The provinces were made responsible for their irrigation works. The central government retained responsibility for income tax, customs duties, salt tax, postal communications and railways, as well as defence and foreign affairs. This division was regarded as a pragmatic delegation rather than a concession of potential **federal** organisation.

At the level of provincial administration, there was perhaps an even more significant division. Matters were deemed to be either 'reserved' or 'transferred'. Reserved matters – characterised as law, order and revenue – would remain the responsibility of the governor's executive council. Transferred matters – characterised as developmental and nation-building – would become the responsibility of the elected legislative council to which provincial ministers would be accountable. For the first time, Indian politicians would hold ministerial power subject to oversight by predominantly Indian councils (see Figure 2.1).

Reserved matters (appointed executive council)	Transferred matters (elected legislative council)
• Land revenue • Law and justice • Police • Irrigation • Labour	• Local self-government (district councils) • Education • Health • Works • Agriculture and cooperatives

Figure 2.1: Provincial government

Reactions

With hindsight, the year 1919 saw the temporary end of anarchic terrorist attacks and the end of military repression. However, it also marked the end of hope for moderate, gradual constitutional change.

Indian nationalist reaction to the 1919 Act was lukewarm. The provisions of the Act were complex and confusing. In fact, an inquiry would be launched in 1924–5 to review the breakdown of the political system created. The Act did not seem worth the prolonged wait during which expectations had built up. There was no point in not taking up the opportunities offered by the Act, but there was a readiness to demand much more. The nationalist movement was about to be transformed from a small political élite pressing for concessions to a genuinely mass protest movement with demands for complete independence.

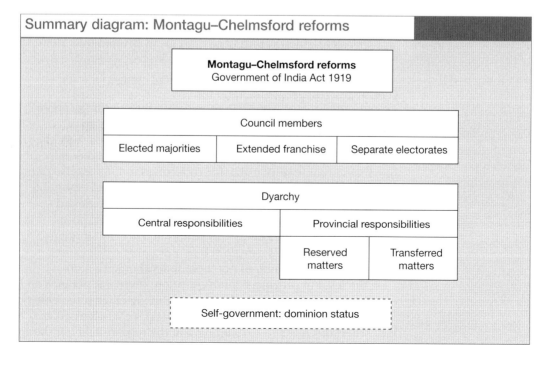

Summary diagram: Montagu–Chelmsford reforms

Study Guide: AS Question

In the style of Edexcel

Source 1

From: a letter written by Motilal Nehru in 1909 to his son, Jawaharlal, commenting on the proposed Morley-Minto reforms. Motilal Nehru was an important member of Congress.

These are not reforms, but a means of destroying the influence of the Indian educated classes in national politics.

Source 2

From: Denis Judd, Empire, *published in 1996.*

The 1909 Indian Councils Act modestly extended the franchise, but quite substantially increased the numbers of elected and nominated Indians on the provincial and central legislative councils of the Raj. The British, by holding out the prospect of progress towards responsible government, were undoubtedly hoping to contain and defuse the forces of Indian nationalism. Thus the extension of democratic institutions was used as a means of shoring up the fundamentally autocratic British Raj.

Source 3

From: Bipan Chandra, India's Struggle for Independence, *published in 1988.*

The real purpose of the Morley–Minto reforms was to divide the nationalist ranks and to check the growing unity among Indians. The reforms introduced a system of separate electorates under which Muslims could only vote for Muslim candidates in constituencies especially reserved for them. This was done to encourage the notion that the interests of Hindus and Muslims were separate and not common.

Use Sources 1, 2 and 3 and your own knowledge.
Do you agree with the view that the real purpose of the Morley–Minto reforms was to 'divide the nationalist ranks'? Explain your answer, using Sources 1, 2 and 3 and your own knowledge. (40 marks)

Exam tips

The cross-references are intended to take you straight to the material that will help you to answer the question.

This is an example of a (b) question, worth two-thirds of the marks for the unit. You should expect to write a substantial answer to this question – leaving yourself about 35–40 minutes to write up your answer after you have analysed the sources and planned a response.

Examiners will award you a maximum of 16 marks for making use of the provided sources and 24 marks for deploying your own knowledge. You must identify points raised by the sources, and then use your own knowledge to develop those further and to introduce new and relevant points which the sources do not contain. But you should start your plan with the sources to ensure that you don't get so carried away with planning and writing a standard essay answer that you forget to use the sources properly. For the highest marks, you should develop techniques which enable you to use your own knowledge in combination with material from the sources – integrating the two.

Try working with a set of columns which allows you to:

- sort your material into that which agrees with the claim in the question and that which counters it
- plan in an integrated way where your own knowledge can extend a point found in the sources.

Some examples are given below.

AGREE (evidence from sources)	AGREE (evidence from own knowledge)	DISAGREE (evidence from sources)	DISAGREE (evidence from own knowledge)
Source 3: The system of separate elections was introduced to encourage the notion that the interests of Hindus and Muslims were not common			
		Source 2: The Act extended the democratic institutions within India, substantially increasing the number of elected and nominated Indians on provincial and central legislative councils. Its purpose was to make concessions in order to 'contain and defuse the forces of nationalism'	

AGREE (evidence from sources)	AGREE (evidence from own knowledge)	DISAGREE (evidence from sources)	DISAGREE (evidence from own knowledge)
			The reforms aimed to produce better-informed and more effective government by the British (page 40)

Additional points are given below. Try slotting these remaining points into a plan. You will need to decide into which column they should go and how they should be grouped. Do some of them add to points in the plan above, or are they new points?

Can evidence to support them be found in the sources, from the sources with additional material from your own knowledge, or do they come entirely from your additional knowledge gained from Chapter 2?

- The reforms aimed to reduce the nationalist influence (Sources 2 and 3).
- The reforms were not planned to lead to an Indian parliament or self-government in the foreseeable future (page 40 and Source 2).
- The partition of Bengal had aroused Hindu fury and led to Muslim fears of Hindu political dominance if Indians were allowed self-government (page 39).
- Lord Minto was sympathetic to the demands of the Simla delegation for separate Muslim electorates (page 40).
- Some historians see Minto's aims as trying to encourage a loyal Muslim political strength to counterbalance the growth of Congress (page 40).
- The British government was alarmed by agitation over the partition of Bengal and support for *swadesh* (page 40) and wished to increase the contact between the administration of government in India and public opinion in India.
- The purpose of the reforms was to bring in a cross-section of public opinion and this could only be done by reserving numbers of seats for specified groups (page 41 and Source 1).

Now that you have sorted and grouped the relevant points, what is your decision? What do you see as the real purpose of the Morley–Minto reforms?

3 Campaigns and Concession 1919–39

POINTS TO CONSIDER

For India, the period between the two world wars is stamped with the personality of Mahatma Gandhi. He brought a new style to Indian nationalism involving the mass of the people rather than an educated élite. He adopted the tactics of peaceful protest and added a spiritual dimension which the British found difficult to deal with. They found their preference for meetings and conferences out of touch, their legislation was too little too late and the punishment of imprisonment was turned into a badge of honour. At the end of the period, Congress triumphed in the first real elections in India, but their high-handed treatment of Muslim politicians encouraged the growth of separatist politics initiated and exploited by the British.

This chapter examines in more detail:

- Gandhi's principles, campaigns of civil disobedience and the British responses
- Demands for and resistance to dominion status
- Major political concession in the Government of India Act 1935
- Elections and relations between Congress and the Muslims

Key dates

1919–21		Non-cooperation campaigns
1922	February 6	End of non-cooperation
1928		Simon Commission in India
	August	Nehru Report presented all-parties conference
1929		Dominion Declaration by British government
1930	March 12	Start of the Salt March
	November 12	First round table conference
1931	March 5	Gandhi–Irwin Pact
	September 7	Second round table conference
1932	August 4	British government's communal award
1933–4		Individual civil disobedience
1935	August 2	Government of India Act
1937		Indian general election

1 | Gandhi and Non-cooperation

Introduction

Key question
Why did Gandhi become a national figure?

Mohandas Karamchand Gandhi was propelled to national stature by the reaction to the Rowlatt Act and the Amritsar Massacre and by capturing popular imagination through his style of campaigning. Before then Gandhi was a promising but no longer youthful politician in the Congress Party which itself remained a middle-class organisation for proposing constitutional change. Within a few years, Gandhi's campaigns had galvanised public opinion in India and Britain and had succeeded in bringing support to Congress from the masses of India.

Gandhi's methods were a powerful combination of spiritual strength, political skill and sheer theatricality. He was one of the great figures of the twentieth century and will be forever associated with the concepts of non-violent protest and civil disobedience. He was not the first to develop or practise this approach, but his various campaigns drew international attention because of the complex problems they caused the British. They were often unsuccessful in their precise objectives but there is agreement that, overall, Gandhi's genius was to recognise that the British Empire could be defeated by mass peaceful passive confrontation. His campaigns exposed the fact the Empire survived because of Indian support and if that was withdrawn, it could not continue.

Key date
Non-cooperation campaigns: 1919–21

Gandhi led five national campaigns of civil disobedience, in addition to more personal interventions such as fasts. The campaigns are now known as:

- 1919 non-cooperation movement
- 1921 non-cooperation movement
- 1930 Salt March and civil disobedience campaign
- 1932 civil disobedience campaign
- 1942 Quit India movement.

Gandhian principles

The principles which guided Gandhi's campaigning, and their effect on political actions, require preliminary explanation.

Satyagraha

Key term
Satyagraha
Literal meaning is truth-force or soul-force.

Satyagraha is the root concept which Gandhi developed through his legal campaigning work for Indians in South Africa. He described it as 'not predominantly civil disobedience but a quiet and irresistible pursuit of truth.'

Satyagraha requires individual campaigners to commit their emotional and spiritual conviction to the struggle for truth and overall justice. This involves the rejection of dishonourable motives such as campaigning for the advantage of one religious community over another. It also involves a generally ascetic lifestyle and a willingness to suffer for the cause, either by placing oneself in the path of physical violence or by engaging voluntarily in painful symbolic actions such as hunger strikes. Either of these might lead to death.

Satyagraha is itself developed out of Hindu philosophy of *dharma*: the need to take right action in the world. The word emphasises force rather than passivity.

Ahimsa

Ahimsa develops a practical and political method out of *satyagraha*.

In a political campaign for independence, peace and justice, it is unacceptable to use provocative or retaliatory violence. Accordingly, the campaign methods used involve inaction, withdrawal of cooperation, resignations, hartals, boycotts or even just silence. In the face of physical force, campaigners must submit with dignity, relying on the moral effect of their suffering to provoke guilt in the attacker and a crisis of conscience and determination.

Ahimsa shows Gandhi's willingness to adapt ideas from other religions since it clearly relates to the Christian concepts of loving one's enemies and turning the other cheek.

Swadesh

Swadesh pre-dates Gandhi's political prominence. *Swadesh* emerged as a response to the 1905 partition of Bengal in a commitment to abstain from the purchase of British goods.

It is entirely Gandhian in its dignified avoidance of a particular action, even at personal cost or discomfort. Gandhi, however, took it further. He urged supporters, and required his close followers, to learn how to spin cloth and to spend an hour a day spinning in order to increase personal and national economic self-reliance. Clothes made of home-spun cloth, **khadi**, became a sign of political commitment especially at high-level negotiations. From 1921, Gandhi himself chose to wear the peasant **dhoti**.

Swadesh is part of Gandhi's vision of a return to a medieval economic system of **cottage industry**.

Swaraj

Gandhi had written a book while in South Africa entitled *Hind Swaraj* (Indian Self-rule). He would declare *swaraj* as a political goal in his first campaigns and the Swaraj Party was formed in 1923.

The 1919 non-cooperation movement

Gandhi's first interventions in India were in two industrial disputes in Bihar and in Gujarat. The Bihar campaign on behalf of workers in the indigo trade was a notable success.

In 1919, Gandhi gained a narrow majority in Congress for a national campaign of protest about the Rowlatt Act and the Amritsar Massacre. The movement swelled into a loosely organised protest movement, the first non-cooperation

Key terms

Ahimsa
Literal meaning is non-violence.

Khadi
Home-spun cloth or clothing.

Dhoti
Loin cloth.

Cottage industry
Pre-factory organisation of home weaving or workshops, for example.

Profile: Mohandas Karamchand Gandhi; later Mahatma ('Great Soul') Gandhi 1869–1948

1869	– Born in Porbander, western India
1888	– Became a law student in London
1893	– Practised as a lawyer in South Africa
1915	– Received the Kaiser-i-Hind war medal for ambulance work
1915	– Returned to India
1919–48	– Active in political campaigning
1948	– Assassinated

Mohandas Gandhi has been described by historian Patrick French as: 'The most famous Indian since the Buddha and the most influential political campaigner of the twentieth century.'

Gandhi's writings and others about him amount to an estimated 30 million words.

Gandhi was born, the youngest of six, into the Bania caste in the Gujerat region. Banias are typically grocers and the term is sometimes used to imply a selfish bargainer. In fact, his father was chief minister at the court of an Indian prince. He was married in 1882 to Kasturba and later had four sons. While studying law in London he lived a frugal life devoted to vegetarianism. On his return to India he found he was hopelessly nervous as a barrister in court. So he left for South Africa, which had a large Indian population, for a year.

When in South Africa, he was thrown off a train for being Indian and committed himself to work against racial discrimination. It was in South Africa that he developed his ideas for political campaigns. In 1906, he committed his first act of *satyagraha*: refusing to register under the racial pass laws.

Gandhi returned to India in January 1915 with a considerable reputation. He was taken under the wing of Gokhale and advised to spend a year touring the country to understand problems and politics. Gandhi set up a *satyagraha ashram* at Ahmedabad. In 1917, he intervened successfully in the protest in Bihar by indigo workers.

Gandhi was at first motivated by a desire for Hindu–Muslim friendship and unity. He also campaigned ceaselessly for the inclusion of the so-called untouchables – the lowest caste – declaring them *harijans* or sons of god. However, he could be naïvely condescending and came close to stating that Muslims would eventually become Hindus. He was always wilfully contradictory and inconsistent in both statements and political tactics. Over time, his political objectives gradually became more inflexible. Most commentators agree that his rejection of Western values and of the entire concept of progress were actually counter-productive in the final stages of the independence movement.

Historian Judith Brown has commented: 'It is almost impossible at this distance of time to understand how Gandhi's mind was working.'

Gandhi's political ideas were enmeshed with a cluster of ideas and personal practices concerning health, diet and sex. For example, from 1906, he abstained from sexual intercourse with his wife for the rest of his life in order to preserve his energy and focus for *satyagraha*. Not content with this, however, he adopted the practice in old age of sleeping naked with female supporters in order to test his celibacy.

Gandhi's ripostes could be withering. Dressed only in his shawl and loincloth, he met George V at Buckingham Palace, no doubt dressed to the imperial nines. When asked by reporters if he had been appropriately dressed, Gandhi responded that the King-Emperor had been wearing enough for both of them.

Famously, when asked what he thought of Western civilisation, Gandhi replied that he thought it would be a good thing.

Gandhi's autobiography, entitled *The Story of My Experiments with Truth*, has been described as Victorian sermonising. More recommended is Bhikhu Parekh: *Gandhi, A Very Short Introduction*. Patrick French's narrative history *Liberty or Death* is refreshingly candid about Gandhi's effectiveness and scathing of the famous biopic *Gandhi* directed by Richard Attenborough.

movement, largely consisting of *hartals*. Gandhi also returned his war medals to the government.

Khilafat

Gandhi also linked the protest with the **Khilafat**, a Muslim movement of grievance.

Khilafat
Campaign to protect the last link with the medieval caliphs or deputies of the prophet Muhammad.

Key term

The Ottoman Empire, ruled by the sultan, the last in a 1000-year history of caliphs, had been defeated in the First World War. The British and French were proceeding to break up the empire, creating new states such as Turkey and Iraq. The position of the sultan was precarious and this was perceived as an attack on the international Muslim community.

In India, Muslim opinion had turned against the British, not least because it was the British who had removed the last Mughal emperor in 1858. Gandhi, genuinely concerned about the sense of Muslim grievance, spoke at Khilafat conferences. In 1920, Congress passed a resolution in support. Even the viceroy, Lord Reading, had argued with the British government over the issue.

The Khilafat movement combined with the general Indian non-cooperation movement to create a powerful sense of anti-British Hindu–Muslim unity. It would not last, however.

The 1920 non-cooperation movement

At the Nagpur meeting of Congress, held in December 1920, Gandhi's proposal for an even larger non-cooperation movement was unanimously approved. Disgust at British popular support for General Dyer, perpetrator of the Amritsar Massacre, turned into support for Gandhi's call for 'a peaceful rebellion'.

Key question
How did Gandhi mobilise for success?

Gandhi declared the aim of *swaraj* within one year, a barely realistic objective but one which touched the mass of Indian population which had hitherto left politics to a middle-class élite.

The protest campaigns included boycotts of law courts by lawyers, of schools and colleges by teachers, and in general of elections, councils, official functions and honours. *Swadesh* was promoted and alcohol prohibited within the movement. A boycott of British cloth had an economic effect on British manufacturers.

Boycotts became huge demonstrations during the visit to India by the Prince of Wales in 1921. Thirty thousand people were arrested. Agitation was rising across the whole country.

It was now apparent that Gandhi was not only the successor to the departed leaders of Congress, Gokhale and Tilak, but also able to create mass support through imagination and symbolism. Even more importantly, he opened up a new kind of politics between the failed approaches of pleading for constitutional concessions and counter-productive terrorist attacks. Gandhi's methods were non-violent but assertive. They did not rely on the rather humiliating notion of proving that educated Indians were becoming able to govern. They gave the masses a part to play with pride.

As the disturbances grew, some Indian leaders, including Jinnah, tried to get the viceroy to find a political way forward. He was sympathetic to the idea and proposed a **round table conference**. Gandhi, however, demanded the release of all prisoners jailed during the protests, including Khilafatists. The viceroy refused and the plan fell through.

Key term

Round table conference
A meeting of comprehensive inclusion with all opinions equally considered.

Key question
Why did Gandhi suddenly abandon non-cooperation?

The end of non-cooperation

At the Ahmedabad session of Congress in December 1921, it was agreed to launch a mass civil disobedience campaign unless the issues of the Khilafat and the Amritsar Massacre were redressed. As this third campaign got under way, Gandhi suddenly called it off as a result of growing communal violence.

The Moplah rebellion

A rebellion had already broken out, early in 1921, in the Malabar region, largely populated by the Moplahs, descendants of the earliest Muslim Arab traders. Unrest was common but the agitation caused by the non-cooperation movement and the Khilafat (or their lack of success, according to some) was exacerbated by resentment of rich local landlords. A small altercation led to police reinforcements, further resentment and rioting.

At this point, the Moplahs turned on their Hindu neighbours. Over 600 were killed and 2500 forcibly converted to Islam. The provincial government called in troops and martial law was ruthlessly imposed in a prolonged rerun of the Amritsar situation. Over 2000 rebels were killed, including 66 left to suffocate in a train wagon.

The ominous character of the communal violence cast a shadow over the non-cooperation and nationalist movement.

Chauri Chaura

And then at the height of the campaign, on 6 February 1922, Gandhi declared the movement over. He was personally devastated that, the day before, a protest mob in the town of Chauri Chaura had burned to death 22 policemen. For Gandhi the moral imperative was clear. A non-violent movement must be just that or nothing. He announced: 'Let the opponent glory in our so-called defeat. It is better to be charged with cowardice than to sin against God.'

Key date

End of non-cooperation: 6 February 1922

For his supporters, both Hindu and Muslim, this was a betrayal of the movement. It left Congress split. The Khilafatist Muslims were even more demoralised when Turkish nationalists, led by Kemal Ataturk, swept to power in 1922, but promptly abolished the monarchy in the name of modernisation, leaving the sultan powerless and irrelevant.

Gandhi remained firm. Indeed, he declared his intention of removing himself from political campaigning, saying that he intended to work on regenerating the moral culture of India from his **ashram** at Sabarmati.

Key term

Ashram
Small religious, often farming, community.

Before he could devote himself to this programme, however, he was arrested by the British on 10 March 1922 and sentenced to six years' imprisonment for sedition.

However, the arrest of tens of thousands during the campaigns had turned imprisonment into a badge of honour. The Indian masses were no longer afraid of British legal authority.

Summary diagram: Gandhi and non-cooperation

```
               ┌──────────────────────────────┐
               │            Gandhi            │
               ├───────────────┬──────────────┤
               │ Five campaigns │ Four principles │
               └───────────────┴──────────────┘
                          │
                  ┌───────────────┐
                  │    Khilafat    │
                  └───────────────┘
                          │
              ┌───────────────────────┐
              │ Moplah; Chauri Chaura  │
              └───────────────────────┘
                          │
          ┌───────────────────────────────┐
          │ Gandhi calls off non-cooperation │
          └───────────────────────────────┘
```

Key question
How did the Tory
government try to
prevent reform?

2 | Lord Simon and the Salt March

Gandhi was released in 1924 on medical grounds (suspected appendicitis). He was in no mood, however, for returning to national politics and retired to the *ashram* to concentrate on other matters.

Without his leadership, or perhaps taking advantage of his absence, Indians resumed office in the various councils, encouraged by the viceroy, Lord Reading.

In 1924, Reading was succeeded by Lord Irwin. Irwin would prove to be a skilful negotiator when Gandhi returned to political campaigning in 1930.

During 1924–5, the Muddiman Committee investigated the problems becoming apparent in the political system of dyarchy set up by the 1919 (Montagu–Chelmsford) Act (see page 54). The majority report agreed that the system was 'complex' and 'confused', but concluded that it was too soon to decide on more reform. The minority report declared that the system had 'no logical basis [and was] rooted in compromise and defensible only as a transitional expedient'.

Also in 1924, Lord Birkenhead was appointed as the new secretary of state. He made no secret of his antipathy to the Montagu–Chelmsford reforms. However, he also rejected the criticisms made in the minority Muddiman report and declared that the majority report showed no change was necessary.

Nevertheless, a key feature of the 1919 reforms had been the promise of a review after ten years, scheduled for 1929. Birkenhead feared that, if the Tory government was replaced by Labour in elections before then, further reform would indeed follow.

The Simon Commission

Accordingly, Birkenhead brought forward the review so that it could take place under his control. That control was evident in 1927 in his choice of people appointed to the review group, known as the Simon Commission after its chairperson, Lord Simon. The commission did not contain a single Indian. So, before any discussion, let alone recommendation, it was clear that progress was unlikely.

Key date
Simon Commission in
India: 1928

When the Simon Commission arrived in India in 1928 on a fact-finding tour, the response of Congress was to boycott all meetings and hold protest demonstrations. The Muslim League, led by Jinnah, also avoided the commission. But the commission met other Muslim representatives, which Birkenhead publicised to try to disturb the Hindus and break the boycott.

The commission's work and eventual report was overtaken by two more radical statements: the Nehru Report and the Dominion Declaration.

The Nehru Report

The boycott of the Simon Commission drew Indian political parties closer again. In 1928, an all-parties conference was convened: an Indian-only round table conference. Representatives attended from Congress, the Khilafat Committee, Central Sikh League, the Indian (Princely) States' Subjects Association, the **Parsi** *Panchayat*, the Bombay non-Brahmin Party, the **Communist** Party of Bombay and the Bombay Workers and Peasants Party.

The conference appointed a committee to draw up the principles of an Indian constitution. The chairman was Pandit Motilal Nehru, by whose name the final report is known.

After some difficulty, the Report of the Committee by the All Parties Conference to determine the principles of the constitution of India was presented in August 1928 to the fourth session of the all-parties conference in Lucknow, which approved its recommendations.

The nation would be called the 'Commonwealth of India' and the recommendations were based on gaining dominion status. Despite broad agreement, the radical wing of Congress, led by Jawaharlal Nehru (son of the chairman Motilal) and Subhas Chandra Bose, saw this as a disappointment.

The recommendations also included:

- No state religion; freedom of conscience and practice of religion.
- Joint mixed electorates for lower houses in central and provincial legislatures.
- Reservation of seats for Muslims on central councils and in minority provinces, with Hindu reservation in the North West Frontier Province.
- No reservation of Muslim seats in Punjab and Bengal.
- Reservation of seats for ten years only.
- Universal adult suffrage.

Such all-India agreement was encouraging to nationalists and the conference enthusiastically reappointed the committee to move on from this framework to the painstaking work of drafting a constitution which could be presented as a parliamentary bill. This proved a step too far. First, the idea of a bill was dropped and it was agreed that the report, slightly expanded, was impressive enough.

Then, at the All Parties Convention in Calcutta (late 1928 into 1929), Jinnah, speaking for the All-India Muslim League, clashed with Jayakar of the All-India Hindu *Mahasabha*. Jinnah was arguing for preservation of the spirit of the Lucknow Pact (see page 47) by retaining Muslim reservation of seats in the Punjab and Bengal and one-third of the total seats in the central legislature. Jayakar urged the conference not to start undoing the report and questioned whether Jinnah was sufficiently supported by Muslim opinion.

Key question
How did Indians envisage the final constitution?

Key terms

Parsi
Ancient Iranian religion.

Panchayat
Assembly (originally of five village elders).

Communism
The political philosophy of a classless society with workers in power; ideology of the Soviet Union.

Mahasabha
Literally meaning great association.

Key date

The Nehru Report: August 1928

Key question
Why did the
agreement unravel?

At a subsequent meeting of Congress, the Nehru Report was warmly received, particularly by Gandhi. Jinnah told Congress that sympathetic statements were not enough. There must be legal protection of the position of minorities. He argued that concessions in order to preserve nationalist unity should come from the majority power, Congress, not the minorities.

When Congress rejected his arguments, Jinnah regarded it as a plan to exclude Muslims from the mainstream movement, prompted by their lack of united representation.

Jinnah's hopes of an all-community nationalist movement faded. In March 1929, he made a counter-proposal for a federal constitution with protection for Muslims. This is sometimes called Jinnah's Fourteen Points in a reference to President Woodrow Wilson's postwar principles. However, even the Muslim League rejected this direction. Jinnah decided to retire from politics and indeed leave India for England. However, like Gandhi from South Africa, he would return stronger and more determined.

This marked the end of the short-lived political convergence. Gandhi would soon retake the propaganda initiative and the British would make a series of political concessions. But the Nehru Report went no further and the next piece of British legislation – the 1935 Government of India Act – did not draw on its recommendations.

The Dominion Declaration

The Simon Commission had never been likely to produce progressive findings, but Birkenhead laid down the limits anyway He ruled out any reference to dominion status, even as the ultimate goal of British policy, since this would concede the right of the nation to decide its own destiny and in his words:

> We were not prepared to accord India at present or in any way prejudge the question whether it should ever be accorded.

Key date

Dominion Declaration:
1929

Birkenhead may not have been prepared for that but his political instincts had been right. In 1929, a Labour government came to power and promptly announced plans for a round table conference. It also authorised the Viceroy Lord Irwin to declare that:

> His Majesty's Government saw the attainment of dominion status as the logical outcome of the Montagu declaration of 1917.

British control would be retained over viceregal and military matters but provincial administration would be entirely Indian.

The defeated Tory Prime Minister Stanley Baldwin supported the declaration in order to reassure Indian public opinion that it was agreed national policy and not a party-political tug-of-war.

However, Birkenhead, no longer secretary of state, was outraged because the declaration (and the round table conference) pre-empted any recommendations of the Simon Commission and indeed rendered it irrelevant.

Profile: Jawaharlal Nehru; later Pandit ('Teacher') Nehru 1889–1964

1889	– Born in Allahabad, northern India
1904	– Educated at Harrow public school in England
1907	– Cambridge University, then trained as a barrister
1921	– First imprisonment
1929	– President of Congress
1946	– Head of interim government; Vice-President Governor General's Executive Council
1947–64	– Prime minister of India
1964	– Died

Jawaharlal 'beautiful jewel' Nehru was born into a prosperous Kashmiri Brahmin family. His father, Motilal, was an intellectual and politician. He was an only child until he was 11 years old. In 1916 he was married to Kamala (died 1936) and his daughter Indira was born in 1918.

It was the Amritsar Massacre that aroused Nehru's interest in politics. During the non-cooperation movements his concern for the poor grew with his popular appeal. Nehru believed passionately in modern secular democracy, with equal rights for women, and was a lifelong anti-fascist. He has been called 'a Brahmin who loathed caste'. He himself declared: 'I am a socialist and a republican and am no believer in kings and princes or in the order that produces the modern kings of industry'. He wanted independence for India more for the chance to improve the lives of the population than just political pride.

In the 1920s Nehru visited Europe and Soviet Russia, which impressed him particularly. In the 1930s he was horrified by fascist Europe but on a visit to China established good relations with the nationalist leader Chiang Kai-Shek. Between 1931 and 1935, he spent all but six months in prison, which he described as 'the best university'.

Nehru was the protégé of Gandhi, who described him as 'pure as crystal, he is truthful beyond suspicion. He is a knight [without fear, without dishonour]. The nation is safe in his hands.' However, the increasing emphasis Gandhi placed on religion and Hinduism, in particular, strained their relationship. Nevertheless, Gandhi, the visionary, and Nehru, the politician, have been paired with Marx, the thinker, and Lenin, the achiever.

As prime minister of India, Nehru led Soviet-style five-year plans to industrialise the country and massively increase its food production. In foreign affairs he virtually created the non-aligned movement at the United Nations between the West and the Communist bloc. He was bitterly disappointed by the Chinese invasion of India in 1962.

Nehru was a lonely man but much loved – publicly by the Indian masses and privately by the famous – Sarojini Padmaja Naidu, Lady Edwina Mountbatten, Madame Chiang Kai-Shek, and Jacqueline Kennedy.

Nehru's great achievement was to ensure that India was not a Hindu state as a mirror of Muslim Pakistan. However, his refusal to work with the Muslim League after the 1937 elections was a disastrous mistake.

The standard biography is by Akbar: *Nehru, the Making of India*. There is a shorter read by Shashi Taroor: *Nehru, the Invention of India*.

Nehru's daughter Indira later married a Gandhi (no relation) and created a parliamentary Indian dynasty by becoming prime minister. She was assassinated by her Sikh bodyguard in revenge for her ordering an armed assault on Amritsar's Golden Temple in 1984.

More significantly for the future, the announcement roused the anger of Winston Churchill, the future wartime prime minister, whose opposition to Indian nationalism became as implacable as Gandhi's opposition to the British.

The dominion declaration did nothing to hold back the growing radicalism of nationalism in India. Both the British and Congress were concerned by the growing strength of the Communist Party. The British response was to arrest and imprison the leaders for four years. Gandhi's tactic was to propel Jawaharlal Nehru, the socialist and Soviet sympathiser, to Congress leadership in order to avoid splits and challenges.

Purna Swaraj

Key term

Purna swaraj
Total
independence.

At the Lahore session of December 1929, Jawaharlal Nehru, the new president of Congress, declared the goal of **purna swaraj** and spurned the invitation to participate in the forthcoming round table conference.

Congress nominated 26 January 1930 as independence day. This would be the trigger for renewed non-cooperation with the hope of reuniting the nationalist movement while stemming support for the more radical movements led by Subhas Chandra Bose. The Congress working committee agreed at a secret meeting that Gandhi should have the freedom to initiate a civil disobedience campaign when he judged the moment right.

Gandhi, however, was not confident that the time was right for civil disobedience. He was worried about whether the masses would respond but also about the potential for violence. He inclined towards using a selected group of supporters chosen for their absolute, even religious, commitment to non-violence. Above all, he wanted to avoid Congress being held responsible for another Chauri Chaura and more accusations of betrayal if the campaign had to be halted.

Key question
How did Gandhi's
protest succeed?

The Salt March

Gandhi's solution was brilliantly imaginative and has become one of the most famous protest events in history.

He announced that, with 78 carefully chosen supporters, he would walk the 400 km from his *ashram* at Sabarmati to the sea at Dandi beach. The group would collect muddy sea-salt and boil it in order to make it pure and usable.

The apparent point of this campaign was to publicise a boycott of the salt tax, a tax by the British on a basic ingredient of cooking for the poorest as much as anyone. However, Gandhi also wished, as he stated in a letter of intent to the viceroy: 'to convert the British people through non-violence and thus make them see the wrong they have done to India'.

At first, the British response was to treat the planned march as a joke. Then Gandhi held a gathering before the march which drew 75,000 people. On 11 March 1930, the day before the start, Gandhi himself addressed 10,000 at a prayer meeting. The British soon realised that the march was attracting world press attention.

The 78 *satyagrahis* set out the next day. Every day, as well as marching about 20 km, they were expected to spin *khadi*, engage in group prayers, keep a diary and project peacefulness. If they encountered resistance they would submit according to the principles of *ahimsa*.

Accordingly, the march took on the character of a pilgrimage through the physical challenge and pain of walking in the heat of the sun in the hot dry season. The theme was perfectly symbolic, did not threaten Indian economic interests and embraced all religious communities and castes. It appeared to pose no threat to the running of the British Indian Empire while drawing the world's attention to British greed and exploitation.

Key date

Start of the Salt March: 12 March 1930

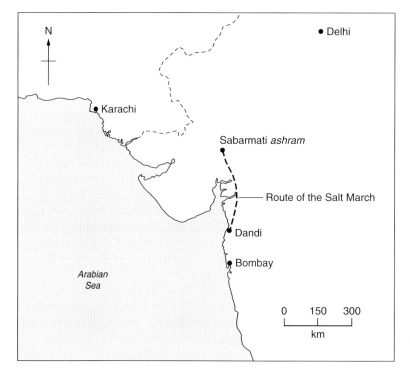

The route of the Salt March of 1929.

Gandhi at the end of his 1930s' Salt March. What moment is captured in the photograph? What might the white clothing suggest to British readers?

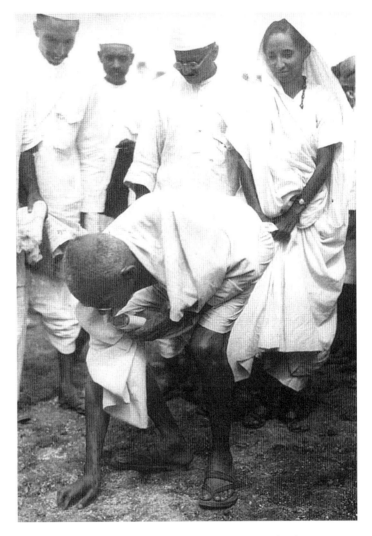

It also challenged the authorities as to how, or whether, to use force against such a peaceful, almost religious, event. On 5 April, the penultimate day of the march, Gandhi declared 'I want world sympathy in this battle of right against might.'

It was also noted, however, that Gandhi's own fear of tensions within the protest group had led to the exclusion of women and the inclusion of just two Muslims.

In towns along the route of the march a large number of Indian officials resigned from their posts. Elsewhere, a march was organised in south India, there were protests in Bombay and the North West Frontier Province and 2000 demonstrators at a salt production plant at Dharasana were attacked by police armed with **lathis**. Two were killed and 320 injured. The international reporting of this showed the dangers of over-reaction.

No direct action was taken against Gandhi and his *satyagrahis* when they reached the sea and the end of their march on 6 April. The police had been ordered to muddy up the salt deposits at the shore but this didn't stop Gandhi creating a lump of salt that he auctioned for 1600 rupees (equivalent to £160 at the time).

Key term

Lathi
A steel-tipped cane.

The propaganda effect was running entirely in Gandhi's favour.
Accordingly, the British felt compelled to take action, even if they
managed to avoid an immediate over-reaction. Over 20,000
protesters were arrested on the viceroy's orders and, on 4 May,
Gandhi himself was arrested under a regulation of 1827 and
taken to Yeravda jail in Bombay.

If the British thought they had now neutralised Gandhi, they
were sorely mistaken.

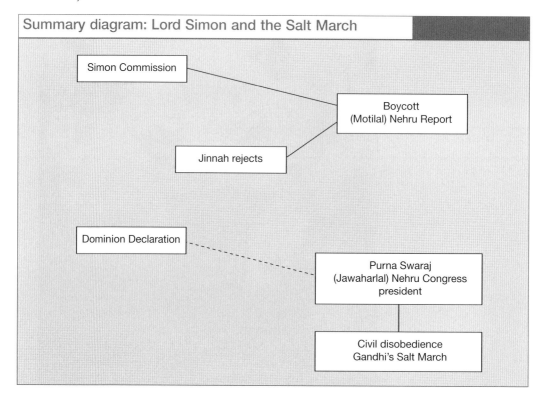

Summary diagram: Lord Simon and the Salt March

3 | Talks

British positions

By the early 1930s, the Liberals had faded and the two main
British political parties were Labour and the Conservatives.
Labour, which had in effect taken on the progressive aims of the
nineteenth-century Liberal Party, was convinced that India was
entitled to democratic autonomy. The Conservatives, as their
name implied, had no desire for change. They accepted the need
for political concessions, if unrest threatened the Empire and
white people in person, but had been generally content that
progress was and would be very slow, with all-party agreement
necessary.

Round table conference

On 31 January 1929, the viceroy, Lord Irwin, had announced that
the Labour government would convene a round table conference
to settle India's constitutional future. This had been followed by
the Dominion Declaration of October 1929.

Key questions
How did the British
proceed?
Were the British
serious?

Indian nationalists naturally assumed that the objective of the conference was to draw up a constitution for the dominion of India. However, the British Liberal and Conservative parties were generally opposed to the granting of dominion status. The government stepped back. Lord Irwin explained to Gandhi, in prison, that the announcement had been merely to reassure about long-term intentions and ensure cooperation with the Simon Commission. Dominion status would not be on offer at the conference. Later the same month, at its Lahore session, Congress responded by agreeing the objective of *purna swaraj* and resolving to boycott the conference.

On 12 November 1930, the round table conference was convened in the House of Lords, London. The conference started with 89 representatives, 16 from the three main British political parties, 16 princes and 57 nominees of the viceroy to represent British India, including Muslims, Sikhs, Indian Christians and **scheduled castes** (termed depressed classes at the conference).

The first session ended in January 1931 with a basic agreement on two points of a future constitutional settlement:

* Central and provincial executive power should be accountable to legislatures (as in modern democracies).
* British India and Indian India (the princely states) should be federally linked as one nation.

However, *The Times*' correspondent summed up the general realisation that 'no Indian delegation without Gandhi, the two Nehrus or Patel could possibly be looked on as representative'. Moreover, so long as Gandhi remained in prison he would be a focus, indeed a cause, of protest and rejection.

Accordingly, in January 1931, Irwin took the bold step of releasing Gandhi in order to undertake personal negotiations. These led to a political agreement which enabled the round table conference to progress but also led to accusations of betrayal on both sides.

The Gandhi–Irwin Pact

The agreement was a formal legal document, signed on 5 March 1931 and publicised the same day.

Known as the Gandhi–Irwin Pact, it stated that, on Gandhi's side:

* The civil disobedience movement would be halted.
* Congress would participate in a reconvened round table conference.

And on Irwin's side:

* An inquiry into police brutality would not be held.
* Political prisoners not guilty of violent crime would be released.
* Banned organisations would be unbanned, fines cancelled, other restrictions lifted and officials re-employed if they had resigned.

- Peaceful picketing in support of Indian goods was permitted, but not when it threatened the sale of British goods.
- The government promised that all future political changes would be in the interests of India itself.

Congress ratified the agreement although there was criticism that yet again the mass movement had been abandoned when it seemed to be getting somewhere. However, it was recognised that the manner in which the pact had come about made Gandhi equal in stature, if not legal status, to the viceroy. The symbolism of this was more important than the detail.

Key question
What did the Gandhi–Irwin Pact achieve?

When Lord Willingdon became viceroy later in 1931, he made no secret of his scorn for Irwin's 'weakness' which now obliged him to treat Gandhi with public respect.

Irwin had, however, recognised the dangers of ever larger and more effective mass movements. He reported to the British government that repression by force would only make matters worse in the long run. Political dialogue was the only safe way forward. He stated his view that:

> What is important is to make perfectly plain to India that the ultimate purpose for her is not one of perpetual subordination in a white Empire.

Churchill's reaction

To the British Conservatives it appeared that the government was rewarding the chief Indian troublemaker for creating disorder. Winston Churchill declared in the House of Commons that it was:

> alarming and also nauseating to see Mr Gandhi, a seditious Middle Temple lawyer, now posing as a fakir of a type well known in the East, striding half-naked up the steps of the viceregal palace while he is still organising and conducting a defiant campaign of civil disobedience to parley on equal terms with representative of the King-Emperor. Such a spectacle can only increase the unrest in India and the danger to which white people there are exposed.

Churchill resigned from his opposition front-bench position specifically to campaign around Britain against Congress. Churchill had grown up surrounded by imperialist beliefs in the superiority of white people and Christian values. He now formed the India Defence League with support from 50 Tory MPs and Lancashire cotton industrialists. His reactionary passion led him to make statements such as that democracy was 'totally unsuited' to Indians. He saw no problem with making it clear to Indians that they would be forever subordinate subjects in a British Empire. This in turn led Prime Minister Stanley Baldwin to declare that the greatest danger to the Empire was 'extremists in India and at home'.

Profile: Winston Spencer Churchill 1874–1965

1874	– Born in Woodstock, near Oxford
1897	– Served as an army officer on North West Frontier
1899–1902	– Saw action in the Boer War, South Africa
1900	– Became a Conservative MP
1905–15	– Served as a Liberal government minister
1914–18	– Saw action on the Western Front and became secretary of state for war
1924–9	– Chancellor of exchequer in the Conservative government
1940–5	– Prime minister during the Second World War
1950–5	– Re-elected prime minister
1965	– Died

Churchill was another of the great figures of the twentieth century. He was born at Blenheim Palace, awarded to his ancestor the Duke of Marlborough for military victories, but he was also the grandson of an American millionaire. He had a speech impediment, did poorly at Harrow public school and suffered from deep depressions.

Churchill threw himself into military action on the borders of the British Empire, combined with journalism. He entered Parliament as a Conservative but switched to the Liberals and soon held high office. He switched back after the war but his opposition to Indian nationalism and his calls to prepare for war against Germany, as well as the changes of party, gave him the reputation of a maverick.

The onset of war vindicated Churchill and he became an inspirational leader but was abruptly kicked out in the 1945 elections because of popular desire for a more equal society. He became prime minister again in 1950, was knighted and US President Kennedy made him the first ever Honorary Citizen of America. On his death Queen Elizabeth II granted him a state funeral that was broadcast on television around the world.

The second and third round table sessions

The round table conference reconvened on 7 September 1931, chaired by the new secretary of state Sir Samuel Hoare.

Gandhi was the only representative of Congress but was **mandated** to make no concessions from the demand of *purna swaraj*. Gandhi did however claim to speak for all India in his sole person, bluntly questioning the right of his fellow Indians to be round the table at all. This naturally provoked anger from the representative of the scheduled castes, Dr Bhimrao Ambedkar, and the three Muslim representatives.

Not surprisingly, then, the second session ended without agreement on the political protection to be given to different religious communities. As a result, the British government announced on 4 August 1932 the communal award setting out

Key date

Second round table conference:
7 September 1931

Key term

Mandated
Instructed by a political organisation.

rights to separate representation for recognised minorities and for the scheduled (or 'depressed') castes. This last point provoked Gandhi to start another fast, on the grounds that Congress, or at least he personally, was the best protector of the dalits, whom he had taken to calling *harijans* in a rather condescending manner.

By the time the third session was convened, the prime minister Ramsay Macdonald had lost the support of his own Labour Party and continued in office only through a National Government formed of his supposed political opponents. Because the Labour Party had been the main driver for Indian political progress, this doomed the final session, which Gandhi and many others did not attend.

British government's communal award: 4 August 1932

Key date

Harijans
Translates as sons of god.

Key term

Civil disobedience

While Gandhi had participated in the second session of the round table conference, the repression of ordinary Indians had continued with particularly brutal measures in Bengal.

When the demoralised Gandhi returned from London, Viceroy Willingdon saw this as the moment to strengthen the weak

Key question
Why did increased repression strengthen nationalism?

Gandhi at the round table conference in September 1931. Given the weather in London at the time, what would Gandhi's choice of clothing suggest to a British newspaper reader?

position Irwin had left him and had Gandhi arrested within a week of his return.

Congress declared that the letter and spirit of the Gandhi–Irwin Pact was broken and requested discussion with the Viceroy. Congress resolved on 1 June 1932 that:

> in the event of a satisfactory response not forthcoming from the viceroy, the Working Committee calls upon the nation to resume civil disobedience, including non-payment of taxes.

Far from giving a satisfactory response, the government granted itself, within 24 hours, emergency powers. It proceeded to outlaw not Congress as such, but the whole of its working organisation, its local branches and committees. An estimated 100,000 people were placed under immediate arrest. The confrontation of a year before was firmly back in place and Nehru described British India as a police state.

Gandhi, fasting in protest at the communal award, was released from prison on health grounds. He promptly advised Congress to end the civil disobedience and requested the government to release the prisoners. Both refused.

Individual civil disobedience

Key date

Individual civil disobedience: 1933–4

In fact Congress made a subtle announcement that individuals should feel free to take responsibility for their own civil disobedience. Between August 1933 and March 1934 thousands took such action while Congress could claim it was not official policy. Gandhi was again arrested but once again released because of his health.

Eventually, the action was crushed by mass arrests and repression but the nationalist movement had lost its fear together with its respect for British justice and values. *Guardian* newspaper correspondent H.N. Brailsford wrote in January 1931:

> To face the *lathi* charges became a point of honour and in a spirit of martyrdom volunteers went out in hundreds to be beaten. They gave a display of disciplined passive courage. The great mass of the people is not in a normal state of mind. It has been roused to a high pitch of sustained exaltation … to anger, it doubts our sincerity and above all it is passionately devoted to its imprisoned leaders.

Moreover, it is clear from the private reports of various viceroys that the nationalists and their civil disobedience were having much greater success than anticipated and no one knew how to deal with Gandhi.

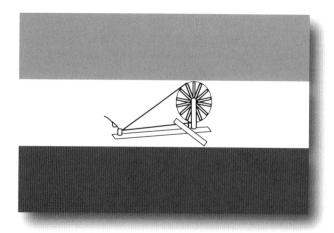

Gandhi's original 1931 design for the Indian flag. The top stripe is saffron (orange) representing Hindus, the bottom stripe green representing Muslims and the central white other faiths. What does the spinning wheel represent in Gandhian thinking? What has the modern Indian flag substituted for the spinning wheel while echoing the original design?

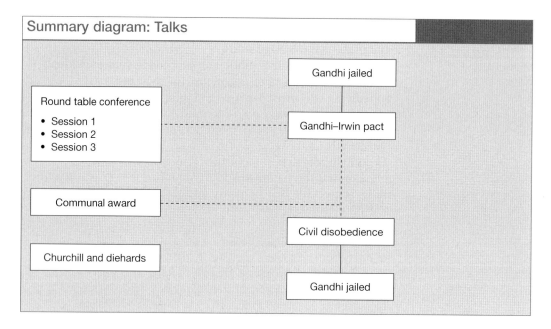

Summary diagram: Talks

Round table conference
- Session 1
- Session 2
- Session 3

Communal award

Churchill and diehards

Gandhi jailed

Gandhi–Irwin pact

Civil disobedience

Gandhi jailed

4 | Elections and Relations Between Congress and the Muslims

The Government of India Act

In 1917 Montagu had declared; in 1929 Irwin had announced. The Simon Commission and the round table conference had come and gone. Resentment in India continued to rise while political progress was stalled. Finally, in 1933 the British government published the long-awaited **white paper** on the Indian constitution.

White paper
A firm set of proposals for legislation.

Key term

The three main principles, based on such agreements as were reached at the round table conference, were as follows:

- eventual federation at the national level
- provincial autonomy
- special responsibilities and safeguards vested in the executive power.

The white paper proposals were drafted as legislation by a joint select committee, which included 21 delegates from British India and the Indian states and was chaired by Lord Linlithgow (soon to become viceroy).

There was considerable opposition to the Government of India Bill not only from predictably outraged Conservative imperialists but also from radicals who thought it did not go far enough. The imperialist die-hards wanted 'no surrender', but presented no alternative policy. Nevertheless, they found enough to say to fill over 4000 pages of *Hansard* objecting to as much as they could on the grounds that it would all lead to inefficiency, nepotism and corruption. This would form a stark contrast with the eventual Independence Bill of 1947.

The Bill received royal assent on 2 August, becoming the Government of India Act 1935. With 450 clauses and 15 schedules it was the longest and most complicated legislation ever passed by Parliament. Even then, it proposed to settle the extent of the franchise by subsequent **orders-in-council**.

And despite all that, it still managed to avoid setting a date for even dominion status.

Provisions of the Act

The main provisions of the Act, which would come into effect in 1937, were to:

- expand the electorate to 35 million people (still less than ten per cent of the population)
- abolish dyarchy and give provincial control to all matters previously 'reserved'
- create full provincial governments each with a legislature and executive
- make no great changes to central administration
- retain viceregal responsibility for defence and foreign affairs
- separate off from 1 April 1937 the province of Burma (which would have its own governor reporting to London)
- carve out two new provinces: Orissa and Sind
- reserve (Section 93) powers for central government after declaration of a state of emergency, including overturning provincial legislation during 'disorder'.

Reaction

The prolonged wait again ensured that Indians would be disappointed by the outcome. As Nanda Saheb, a biographer of Gandhi, has commented:

Key terms

Hansard
Published transcripts of parliamentary debates.

Orders-in-council
Legislation approved by a viceroy without full parliamentary scrutiny.

Key date

Government of India Act: 2 August 1935

> Each instalment tended to become out of date by the time it was actually granted. The reforms of 1919 might well have appeased India in 1909; the reforms of 1935 would have evoked enthusiasm in 1919, etc.

In any case, the full effect of the Act would not come until elections in 1937 so there was a lull in activity. Congress in particular was divided between opposition to the Act in principle and attempting to gain whatever power the Act offered.

Federation and the princes

A major feature of the 1935 Act was the aim of eventual federation of British India and the princely states, once half of the states had agreed.

Although no date had been set for dominion status, it was clear that it would come. So, the British attempted to ensure that a future self-governing dominion had a constitution which would strengthen conservative and loyal elements, limit the control which Congress might seek and increase regional power which might weaken Congress as a national organisation.

Accordingly, along with concessions to the Muslim League, the federation of the princely states was designed to bring into government these natural conservatives. To help persuade them, the Act contained various protections and inducements.

For example, the princes would be permitted to select their own representatives without elections. In addition, although the princely states contained 20 per cent of the population, they would have 33 per cent of the representatives in the lower federal assembly and 40 per cent in the higher council of state.

Nevertheless, the princes refused one by one to sign up to the agreement. They feared too much that there would be pressure to move from their autocratic structures towards democratic processes and to relinquish their personal armies into national armed forces.

Their opposition stalled any moves towards federation and when Britain declared war on Germany in 1939, the initiative was formally suspended.

Nehru observed ironically how eager the 'advanced' Europeans were to work with the most reactionary forces of 'backward' India to thwart progress.

The late 1930s

Between the passing of the 1935 Act and the 1937 elections, there was another change of viceroy. In April 1936, Lord Willingdon was succeeded by Lord Linlithgow, who would turn out to be the longest serving viceroy since Dalhousie in the mid-nineteenth century. And just as Dalhousie's policies had contributed to the causes of the Indian Mutiny (see page 10), so would Linlithgow's reactionary and repressive approach accelerate the complete end of the British Raj.

Viceroy and Vicereine Linlithgow photographed leaving their official residence in 1940 to attend a garden party. To what extent do the clothes represent historical change or continuity?

On the nationalist side, Gandhi remained the prime force. Congress had given the president more power including the choice of members of the Congress working committee. Accordingly, the choice of president was ever more crucial and behind the scenes Gandhi's views were decisive. In 1936, Gandhi ensured that Nehru was elected president for the second time. He had to overcome Nehru's own reluctance because of pressure from leftist Congress socialists to reject the 1935 Act. Nehru's presidency ensured that Congress remained a broad force rather than splintering into squabbling groups.

The 1937 elections

If the 1935 Act had been an anticlimax, the elections of 1937 to the positions created by the Act electrified the political situation.

A sense of Indians governing Indians was palpable and, for the first time, the terms prime minister and council of ministers were used. Within a short period, ministries increased spending on education and public health, while regulating landlords and moneylenders. The ministries worked effectively, distributing and

Key question
How did elections change the political struggle?

Key date

Indian general election: 1937

Profile: Lord Linlithgow 1887–1952

1887	– Born in South Queensferry, West Lothian
1933	– Chairman of the Joint Select Committee on Indian Constitutional Reforms
1936–43	– Viceroy of India
1952	– Died

Victor Alexander John Hope (Hopie), second Marquess of Linlithgow, became the longest-serving viceroy of the twentieth century. At nearly two metres tall, he was also the longest in body. As a result of boyhood polio, he could only turn his head by turning his body which, with his height, gave him an imperious manner.

Linlithgow chaired the committee whose recommendations became the 1935 Government of India Act. He is said to have worked hard to prepare the Indian princes for federation with British India. Nevertheless, his lasting image is of a traditional imperialist toff, partly because of his rigorous suppression of nationalist campaigns and partly, at the end, his refusal to intervene in the Bengal Famine of 1943.

Nehru described him as:

Heavy of body and slow of mind, solid as a rock and with almost a rock's lack of awareness, possessing the qualities and feelings of an old-fashioned British aristocrat, he sought with old integrity and honesty of purpose to find a way out of the tangle.

allocating work with little intervention or obstruction from British governors. Parliamentary secretaries were appointed to start to develop a new generation of political leaders.

In electoral terms, Congress was victorious and took power in Bihar, Bombay, Madras, the United Provinces and the Central Provinces. Congress was now, in effect, the governing party of India. To co-ordinate its approach across the country in the various provincial governments, Congress created the Congress Parliamentary Board (CPB) – in short, a party committee to determine national policy. The chairman of the CPB, Sardar Patel, was therefore the most important politician in the country. Patel ensured that the more radical proposals of the Congress president, Nehru, were aired but then defeated. In the words of a British intelligence report (quoted by French): 'Nehru is the high-grade tool in the hands of the skilled craftsman.'

Reactions

Gandhi became still more distanced from actual politics. On the one hand, he thought the new powers likely to corrupt and distract Indian politicians. On the other, he regarded his own spiritual 'corruption' as responsible for the problems of the country.

Congress felt itself so powerful as a result of the electoral landslide that it refused to cooperate with the viceroy unless he promised not to overrule decisions by provincial governments. The disdainful Linlithgow was eventually forced to agree.

More seriously, the Muslim League was treated with disdain by Congress itself which refused to include any Muslim politicians in provincial governments. The consequences of this refusal, described by Ayesha Jalal as 'one of the gravest miscalculations by the Congress leadership in its long history', would be disastrous for the unity of the country.

The Muslim position

Key question
How did Jinnah move to build up the Muslim League?

Political representation for Muslims was fragmented. There were 482 seats reserved for Muslims in the 1937 elections and the Muslim League was the largest group with only 109. The League held 15 per cent of all the seats in the legislatures, when the Muslim population was 22 per cent. This was a far cry from the dominance of Congress in the open seats. Congress itself, despite Gandhi's claims that it represented all India, had only 26 Muslim representatives out of 1500, less than 2 per cent. Nevertheless, Nehru declared that he came 'into greater touch with the Muslim masses than most of the members of the Muslim League'.

Jinnah, who had been persuaded to return from his successful law work in London to lead the Muslim League, was spurred to action by the results and the refusal of Congress to include Muslim politicians. Jinnah adopted the following strategies:

- He persuaded smaller Muslim organisations to merge with the Muslim League. Maulana Abul Kalam Azad, the leading Muslim within Congress, rejected him and Jinnah denounced him as a puppet of the Hindus.
- After being elected as president in 1937, he reformed the structures of the Muslim League and appointed effective supporters to key positions.
- Despite his own belief in secular politics and states, he began to campaign openly on a separate Muslim basis rather than as part of a nationalist movement.
- Knowing that political Muslims were generally of the landlord and landowner class, he avoided the social radicalism and working-class character of Congress. To further appeal to this class, he promoted the use of the high-class language Urdu, even though he could not speak it himself.
- Increasingly, he identified Congress as the threat to Muslim interests. A popular target was the Congress anthem, 'Bande Mataram', which praised most of the communities of India while pointedly not mentioning the Muslims.
- Finally, Jinnah increasingly moved from the objective of protected Muslim representation within India towards the objective of independent Muslim-controlled provinces or even states. The idea of Pakistan appeared to be a useful negotiation point – whether as promise to Muslims or threat to Congress.

Pakistan

In Lucknow, after the 1937 elections, Jinnah declared his aim to be:

Key question
How did the idea of
Pakistan gain
ground?

> the establishment in India of full independence in the form of a
> federation of free democratic states in which the rights and
> interests of the Musulmans were paramount.

This might be interpreted as the point at which various separatist ideals debated throughout the 1930s were adopted as a political objective.

The poet Muhammad Iqbal had proposed a two-nation future in 1930, allowing Muslims and Hindus their own areas within one Indian state. The two-state idea was crystallised in the name Pakistan, which allegedly came to Choudry Rahmat Ali while on a London bus. On the one hand, the name means 'land of the pure'; on the other, the letters are extracted from the names of the Muslim majority provinces: Punjab, Afghan (North West

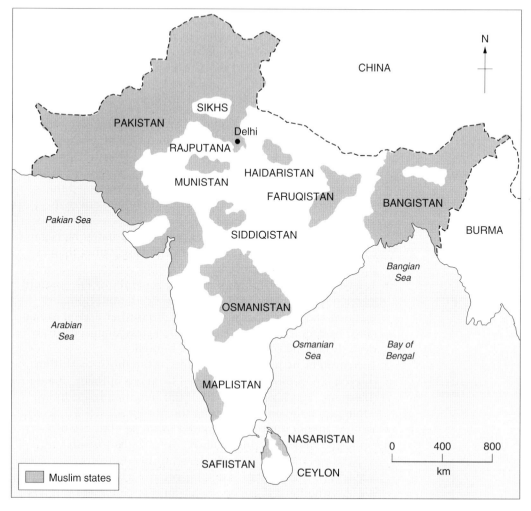

Possible Muslim states across the subcontinent, suggested by Choudry Rahmat Ali, late 1930s.

Profile: Muhammad Ali Jinnah; later Quaid-i-Azam ('Great Leader') 1875–1948

1875	– Born in Karachi, now in modern-day Pakistan
1892–6	– Studied law in England
1909	– Appointed as Congress Muslim representative on Imperial Legislative Council
1913	– Joined the All-India Muslim League
1919	– Resigned over the Rowlatt Act
1929	– Presented the Fourteen Points
1930	– Enjoyed lucrative work as a lawyer in London
1935	– Returned to lead the Muslim League
1940	– Made the Lahore Resolution to demand the formation of Pakistan
1944	– Involved in the Gandhi–Jinnah talks
1946	– Called for direct action as a result of the Calcutta killings
1947	– Became governor-general of Pakistan
1948	– Died

Muhammad Ali Jinnah was born into a lower middle-class family. His father was a merchant.

As a lawyer, Jinnah quickly developed a reputation for devastating effectiveness and gained great wealth as a result. His professional success, reflected in his style of dress and manner, was an important part of his appeal to middle-class Muslims able to vote. The contrast with Gandhi could hardly have been greater.

However, Jinnah's personal life was less happy. His first wife died at a young age. His second wife, Ruttie, was half his age and from a Parsi family, which caused family friction. Ironically, Jinnah would later disown his beloved daughter Dina when she married a non-Muslim. After Ruttie's death in 1929, Jinnah's closest companion was his sister Fatima. From the 1930s onward, Jinnah kept his increasing ill-health a close secret.

Historians recognise two broad phases to Jinnah's political career. Up to the end of the 1920s, Jinnah was a committed Congress nationalist. He was very moderate and disapproved of mass campaigns of disobedience. He was determined to preserve election quotas for Muslims but was personally very secular in outlook. There is considerable evidence that he was not a devout Muslim. He disapproved of Gandhi's mixture of religion and politics.

The Congress rejection of Muslim quotas in the Nehru Report drove Jinnah out of politics (and back to London) for a while. However, the Congress rejection of Muslim politicians after the 1937 elections spurred him to take control, at the request of many Muslims, of the All-India League. Increasingly, Jinnah appeared to support Muslim separatist demands. He started to learn Urdu, which was likely to become the official language of Pakistan, and appeared at public events in formal Muslim clothing. The culmination of this second phase of his career would see Jinnah, uniquely among modern politicians, create almost single-handedly a completely new state formed on a religious basis and become its first supreme leader.

Jinnah is often treated as the villain of Indian nationalism – the wrecker of a united independent India. Much of this comes from his lack of personal charm. Even a friend described him as 'tall and stately, formal and fastidious, aloof and superior of manner'. In Pakistan, however, he is revered as Baba-e-Qaum (Father of the Nation).

Frontier) Kashmir, Sind and Baluchistan. Significantly, Bengal – poor, geographically inconvenient and full of untouchable converts – is missing.

The idea circulated in pamphlets without being taken seriously by either Indians or the British. The practical way forward seemed to be the reservation of seats for Muslims and other minorities as incorporated in British legislation in 1909, 1919 and 1935 and supported by Congress at the Lucknow Pact of 1916. However, the Nehru Report of 1928 and the triumphal scorn of Congress after the 1937 elections showed that this position was precarious in any future Congress-dominated independent India. Muslims and others would have to compete in open democratic processes. The alternative would be to create separate democracies, in other words, split the country. It was the Muslim strategic hope that this would be so unacceptable to Congress that it would preserve the reservation of seats.

In fact, the momentum of the Pakistan movement would become unstoppable because of the obstinate behaviours of both Congress and Churchill during the Second World War.

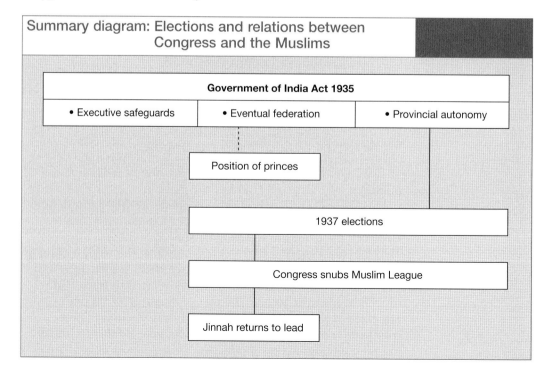

Summary diagram: Elections and relations between Congress and the Muslims

Study Guide: AS Question

In the style of Edexcel

Source 1

From: a declaration written by Gandhi and read out in towns and villages all over India on 26 January 1930.

We hold it to be a crime to submit any longer to [British] rule. We recognise, however, that the most effective way of gaining our freedom is not through violence. We will prepare ourselves by withdrawing all voluntary association from the British government, and will prepare for civil disobedience, including non-payment of taxes. We are convinced that if we can but withdraw our voluntary help and stop payment of taxes without doing violence, even under provocation, the end of this inhuman rule is assured.

Source 2

From: Tim Leadbeater, Britain and India, *published in 2008. Here he is commenting on the views of Lord Irwin in 1931.*

Irwin rightly recognised the dangers of even larger and more effective mass movements. He reported to the British government that repression by force would only make matters worse in the long run. Political dialogue was the only safe way forward. He stated his view that 'What is important is to make perfectly plain to India that the ultimate purpose for her is not one of perpetual subordination in a white Empire.'

Source 3

From: Lawrence James, The Rise and Fall of the British Empire, *published in 1994.*

Even in the periods of intensive public protests in 1919 and 1930–4, it [Congress] had never come close to toppling the Raj or even proving beyond doubt that India was ungovernable. There were no more Amritsars, but the authorities managed to keep the upper hand through mass arrests of leading party activists, including Gandhi, and disorders were held in check by the police with army help. With a loyal police force, the backing of an army which numbered 194,000 in 1939, and a considerable degree of determination among its officials, the Raj was able to hang on without too much strain on its resources.

Use Sources 1, 2 and 3 and your own knowledge.
Do you agree with the view that Gandhi's campaign methods in the 1930s were effective? Explain your answer, using Sources 1, 2 and 3 and your own knowledge.   (40 marks)

Exam tips

The cross-references are intended to take you straight to the material that will help you to answer the question.

You can use your own knowledge (see pages 61–6) in combination with Source 1 to identify the key features of Gandhi's campaign methods at the beginning of the period:

- rejection of British rule
- civil disobedience campaign
- refusal to pay taxes and the associated challenge to the salt tax
- the Salt March
- non-violence
- mass demonstrations.

In order to consider the effectiveness of Gandhi's methods, you can use your own knowledge (see pages 61–79) in combination with Source 2 to show: initial success, political concessions to Gandhi, the Gandhi–Irwin pact and Gandhi's participation in the round table conference.

However, how much had been achieved by 1939? You can use Source 3 and your own knowledge (pages 62–79) to consider limitations to Gandhi's achievements after 1931 and the continuing extent of British control. You should also use your own knowledge of the Government of India Act (pages 80–5) to consider the extent and limitations of nationalist success by 1939.

Note, however, that in spite of the evidence in Source 3 that disorder was contained during the 1930s and British control maintained, the source refers to the British 'hanging on' to control, which itself implies a considerable degree of challenge by 1939.

So, what is your conclusion? How effective were Gandhi's methods in the 1930s?

4

Quit India 1939–45

POINTS TO CONSIDER

The period covering the Second World War marks a crucial change in Indian politics and in Indo-British relations. Nationalists were increasingly angered by the attitude of Churchill, the British wartime leader, who was utterly opposed to further political progress for India. Congress demanded that the British leave India immediately and politicians were imprisoned for preparing civil disobedience in wartime. Congress ordered a complete withdrawal from government. This provided an opportunity for the Muslim League to gain political prominence and appear more loyal. The League adopted a call for a separate state for Muslims, more at first as a way of strengthening their bargaining position than a real plan. The end of war brought a sudden realisation that the British could not hang on to India much longer and planning for independence rapidly gathered speed.

You should gain an understanding of:

- British fears and Churchill's opposition
- The divergence of Congress and the Muslim League
- The role of the anti-British Indian National Army

Key dates

1939	September 3	Start of the Second World War
1940	March	Lahore Resolution
	August	Offer of postwar settlement
1941	August	Atlantic Charter supporting self-government
1942	April	Cripps mission
	August 8	Quit India resolution
1943		Formation of the Indian National Army
	October	Wavell appointed as viceroy
		Suppression of political campaigns
1943–4		Bengal famine
1945	June 25	Simla Conference

1 | Patriotisms

The declaration of war

On 3 September 1939, the British prime minister, Neville Chamberlain, declared war on Germany. On the same day the viceroy, Lord Linlithgow, announced to the Indian people that they too were at war.

It had been obvious that war was coming, which makes it all the more surprising and significant that Linlithgow made his announcement without warning or consultation with Indian political leaders. The manner of the declaration was an affront to the self-respect of all Indians which lasted longer than the war.

Adding insult to injury, the key part of the statement, no doubt intended to strike a resolute note, sounded completely hypocritical to Indian ears. Linlithgow declared that:

> confronted with the demand that she should accept the dictation of a foreign power in relation to her own subjects, India has decided to stand firm.

The British government, especially under the later leadership of Winston Churchill, appeared oblivious to the contradiction of fighting for liberty and democracy while attempting to thwart it for India.

Indian reaction

Nevertheless, over two million Indians would join the armed forces to fight for the cause. Gandhi, meeting Linlithgow on the day after the announcement, was horrified by the idea of Britain under threat. Both he and Jinnah agreed to halt all plans for federation (as laid out in the 1935 Act). Consistent with his views, Gandhi offered to meet Hitler on behalf of Britain to make peace and advised the British that complete **pacifism** was desirable.

However, Nehru and Congress had consistently condemned both fascism and British appeasement of it. They saw no need for sentiment or lectures on loyalty. Linlithgow's arrogant announcement caused great resentment and eight of 11 Congress ministers resigned.

In a pattern to be repeated, this simply provoked British hostility and provided opportunities for Muslim leaders to gain more influence and sympathy. Muslim leaders, for example, declined to make a joint demand with Congress for an early statement of British war aims, which would have forced the issue of comparative liberty and democracy.

The Lahore Resolution

Jinnah sensed that the tide was finally turning in favour of the Muslim League with him in control. In January 1940 he wrote an article arguing for a new constitution because: 'There are in India two nations who both must share the governance of their

Key question
What did the declaration of war reveal?

Key dates

Start of the Second World War:
3 September 1939

Lahore Resolution:
March 1940

Key term

Pacifism
Refusal to fight in wartime.

Key question
How did Jinnah use the concept of nationhood?

common motherland'. He was deliberately raising the stakes by referring to Muslims as a nation rather than a community.

In March 1940 the biggest meeting of the Muslim League so far took place in Lahore. Sixty thousand gathered in a huge tent in Minto Park to hear Jinnah, now dressed in traditional Muslim style, demand the creation of Pakistan. In a significant analogy, he compared the situation of Hindus and Muslims to the relationship of the British and the Irish. He made the ringing declaration that: 'The Musulmans [Muslims] are not a minority. The Musulmans are a nation by any definition.'

Following the logic of this definition, Jinnah demanded much more than complicated voting arrangements for reserved seats. The Muslim League meeting passed a resolution that:

> geographically contiguous units are demarcated into regions which should be so constituted, with such territorial adjustments as may be necessary, that the areas in which the Muslims are numerically in a majority as in the north-western and eastern zones of India should be grouped to constitute 'independent states' in which the constituent units shall be autonomous and sovereign.

Key question
Did Jinnah really want Pakistan to be created?

Ambiguity

The Lahore Resolution was powerfully unclear. It strengthened the unity of the Muslim movement even though it was interpreted differently. Fazlul Huq, one of the drafters and the Muslim leader in Bengal, regarded the phrase 'independent states' as meaning two equal separations, one in the east – Bengal – and one in the west – Pakistan. (This would indeed eventually come to pass in 1971.)

Jinnah, however, let it be known privately that he had only intended two wings to one state. Similarly, the phrase territorial adjustments was not intended to suggest any partition of any province. Moreover, Jinnah also kept open the possibility that the independent Muslim state(s) might still be part of an all-India federal superstate.

The fact that Jinnah did not clarify this publicly until six years later in the Delhi Resolution has raised questions for historians about his true objectives. Jinnah was clearly a secular Muslim. Indeed, he was regarded with suspicion by many Muslims. There is some agreement among historians that he did not truly regard a state based on a religious definition as a wise solution. It follows that he was, like many a politician, arguing tactically for far more than he really thought possible or desirable in order to achieve more than a realistic demand would.

It would later become apparent that the Muslim League, despite being a national organisation, was actually heavily reliant on regional leaders, such as Huq in Bengal. They saw opportunities in the Lahore Resolution to consolidate their power and when the time was right even become national leaders of separate states.

The historian Ayesha Jalal has commented:

> Jinnah's appeal to religion was always ambiguous … evidence
> suggests that his use of the communal factor was a political tactic,
> not an ideological commitment. … Asserting that Muslims were a
> nation avoided the logic of numbers.

The hostage theory

Hindu politicians attacked the resolution over the consequences
for the minorities left out. In the first place there were many
Muslims across India not in the concentrated areas of the north-
west and east. Was it expected that they would move to the new
states or would they become an even weaker minority in an
almost total Hindu state? Similarly, declaring the Muslims to be a
nation entitled to run their own country appeared to overlook the
presence of other religious and ethnic minorities within those
areas, notably Sikhs in the Punjab and Pathans in the North West
Frontier Province.

Jinnah's response came to be known as the **hostage theory**.
This argued rather conveniently and implausibly that the
presence of residual minorities within both Hindu India and
Muslim Pakistan(s) would force each majority to protect the rights
of the minorities within their country for fear of reprisals against
their co-religionists 'left behind' in the other country.

Nehru denounced the Lahore Resolution as 'fantastic'; Gandhi
called it 'baffling', a condescending dismissal since he too made
grand impractical demands as a political tactic.

The British kept quiet, regarding the increasing divergence
between Congress and the Muslim League as a helpful weakness
in the nationalist movement.

Key term

Hostage theory
Vulnerable
minorities in each
country would
ensure mutual
protection.

Churchill as prime minister

In 1940 the war was looking disastrous: France had fallen, the
British army had narrowly escaped destruction during retreat
from Dunkirk and German Luftwaffe raids showed that the Battle
of Britain was underway. In this critical time, the British
government had reached for a new leader and turned to
obstinate maverick Winston Churchill.

Churchill's reactionary views on India were well known. The
secretary of state for India, Lord Zetland, resigned immediately
recognising that his own views, including support for dominion
status, would no longer fit. However, it was Leo Amery, another
previous critic of Churchill, who was eventually persuaded to
become the new secretary, working to a brief of making only the
most limited concessions.

Congress attitudes had been hardening since the Linlithgow
announcement and the British refusal to state war aims. The
government was anxious about a resumption of civil disobedience
that might require deployment of precious armed forces and lead
to unrest within the forces themselves.

Accordingly, Amery attempted to clarify and settle matters by
announcing in the House of Commons that Indian constitutional

Key question
What was Churchill's
attitude?

reform would be resumed after the end of the war. Since this implied nothing before the end of the war, it aroused little support. Linlithgow himself suggested to the war cabinet a slightly more specific offer of guaranteed steps towards dominion status starting one year after the end of the war. The war cabinet rejected it but with good sensitivity. The proposal promised an outcome without involving Indians. The process would need a constituent assembly for democratic approval. However, what this also clearly implied even now was that Muslim demands for a separate state would have to be considered seriously.

August 1940 offer

Churchill was personally against any sort of concession or declaration but eventually permitted Linlithgow to announce in August 1940 the idea of a postwar constitutional settlement.

Too little, too late again, this was rejected by Congress which was looking beyond dominion status. Linlithgow warned the provincial governments that he would crack down heavily on Congress if it initiated civil disobedience which it duly did, calling for individual actions again rather than a mass national campaign.

Swathes of arrests followed and some 20,000 Indians were imprisoned within a year. Linlithgow asked for emergency powers to declare Congress an illegal, even potentially treasonable, organisation. Although Churchill refused, he liked Linlithgow's hardline approach and asked him to continue as viceroy beyond the normal term of office.

The Indian National Army

The question of treason was more stark in the case of the Indian National Army (INA). The INA was formed and led by Subhas Chandra Bose. Bose had been a leading politician in Congress until Nehru was made president.

In 1941 Bose was under house arrest, having recently been released from prison. He took the decision to leave India in order to fight for its independence from abroad. He planned to recruit an army of liberation and for this he was more than willing to work with his enemy's enemy, Nazi Germany. In disguise with false papers at first, he was smuggled out to Afghanistan and then travelled to Berlin.

In Germany, he met fascist leaders such as Ribbentrop and Mussolini, recruited a few thousand Indian prisoners of war (out of 17,000 in Europe) to his Indian legion and held marches behind a newly designed flag. He established the Free India Centre and made radio broadcasts in Indian languages. The Nazis were more interested in this propaganda work than unrealistic ideas about invading India.

Bose realised the situation after a personal meeting with Hitler and took up the offer of submarine passage to Japan in 1943. There he found the Japanese leader General Tojo more supportive.

Key dates

Offer of postwar settlement: August 1940

Formation of the Indian National Army: 1943

Key question
Were Indian National Army soldiers traitors to the Empire or freedom fighters?

Second World War propaganda cartoon. It is possible to identify three powers represented by flags, dress or markings on aircraft. Judging by the script, to whom is the cartoon directed?

Bose meeting German leader Adolf Hitler in 1942. How might such a picture be used by the British? How would Nehru have reacted?

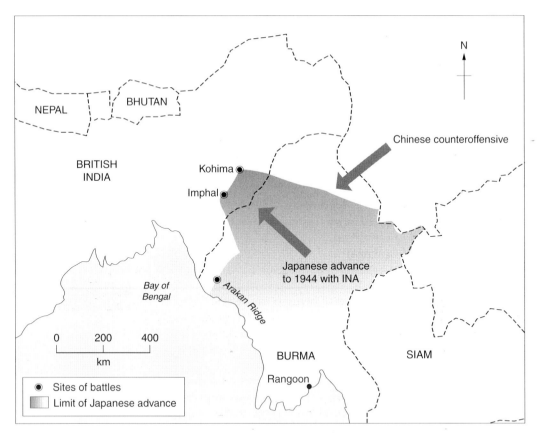

Japanese advance in Burma, showing battles involving the INA in 1944.

Again Bose made propaganda broadcasts ending with the slogan *Dilli Chalo!* (On to Delhi!), the cry of the mutineers in 1857. Across the far east, Bose was able to recruit from two million Indian prisoners of war. Ten thousand volunteered for the newly created INA, although there are unresolved questions about the use of torture on officers and others who might give financial support.

Action against the British

Eventually, the INA reached somewhere between 15,000 and 50,000, including a complete women's regiment. They had a headquarters in Rangoon, Burma, and were given the captured Andaman Islands as independent Indian territory. They were sent into action against the British at the battles of Arakan, Imphal and Kohima. However, they were pitifully supplied and armed and were decimated. Thousands surrendered then, with complete surrender following the capture of Rangoon in 1945. Bose escaped to the island of Taiwan, but died in an air crash.

Bose and the INA were never really a military danger, although it turned out the British had underestimated their military strength. The threat came from their power to provoke unrest within India itself both during the war and afterwards, when the question arose as to how to deal with captured INA soldiers.

There is evidence that many soldiers joined up simply in order to get out of prisoner of war camps, especially those run brutally by the Japanese, and cross over to British forces as soon as they could. Many were desperate to get back because of the famine affecting Bengal from 1943 onwards.

Profile: Subhas Chandra Bose 1897–1945

1897 – Born in Cuttack, eastern India
1917 – Studied at Cambridge University
1924 – First imprisoned for three years
1928 – Created uniformed, armed Congress Volunteer Force
1930 – Mayor of Calcutta
1938 – President of Congress
1945 – Died in a plane crash while flying to Taiwan

Subhas Chandra Bose was proud of being born Bengali, Hindu and Aryan and he enjoyed the experience of white servants at Cambridge. Having been expelled for rebellion at school, he refused to join the Indian Civil Service when he passed the exams.

During the 1920s he visited Ireland and identified with the Irish nationalist cause. In the early 1930s, Bose was imprisoned without trial on suspicion of supporting revolutionaries.

Bose rose to prominence within Congress with further honourable spells in prison. He was released in 1933 on condition that he quit India. He travelled around Europe, meeting leaders and studying politics.

After returning to India in 1936, Bose spent more time in prison but also became mayor of Calcutta and, with Gandhi's support at first, president of Congress, despite disagreement with Gandhi's reactionary views on women, non-violent methods and general lack of clarity. When Gandhi preferred Nehru, Bose was sidelined and he formed the Forward Bloc to oppose mainstream Congress.

Bose himself made no secret of his opposition to the racist ideologies of the fascist regimes whose support he was seeking. However, he was also happy to accept the luxurious lifestyle the Nazis laid on for him.

Bose is now a national Indian hero, particularly in Bengal, where Kolkatta International Airport is named after him. He ranks alongside the Gujarati Gandhi and the Brahmin Kashmiri Nehru as a patriot and creator of independence. Crucially, it is seen in his favour that he actually tried to fight the British and is not tarnished by the mess of partition.

Many Indians believe there was no aircrash in 1945. His life and death are becoming the stuff of legend.

Summary diagram: Patriotisms

Declaration of war

Lahore Resolution

Churchill's August 1940 offer

Bose and INA

2 | Quit India Campaign

The war situation

Key question
How did the USA
view the British
Empire in India?

At the start of 1942, although the threat of invasion had passed, the war was still going badly for the British. The country was on rations, in blackout and under siege from submarines in the Atlantic Ocean and Luftwaffe bombing, while British armies continued to retreat in North Africa. Then came a series of major losses in the east. The most traumatic was the surrender of the fortress city of Singapore combined with the destruction of two major battleships. Japanese armies swiftly occupied British territory in Malaya and Burma. They were pressing at the north eastern border of India itself. It was quite possible that the mighty British Empire would be conquered.

Churchill was acutely aware that Britain's survival rested on the strategic support of the United States. Although the USA did not enter the war until December 1941, it had been providing assistance to Britain by lending ships to get supplies across the Atlantic. The US president, Franklin Delano Roosevelt, had from the start argued with Churchill about the situation of India. It was more than just a matter of protecting the military position by avoiding unrest in India. It was the question of the purpose of the war which Indian nationalists had themselves raised. In a sense, Churchill was to find himself fighting a political war on two fronts – in India and in the USA – even as the Allies planned the opening of a second front against Germany through the invasion of Europe.

The Atlantic Charter

Key date

Atlantic Charter
supporting self-
government:
August 1941

In August 1941, Churchill and Roosevelt had agreed the basis of their cooperation in the Atlantic Charter which included support for 'sovereign rights and self-government'. The two interpreted this differently, however. Churchill regarded it as applying to countries which had been conquered whereas the *status quo* would apply to Britain and its empire. Roosevelt saw it as a fundamental principle applying to all. Accordingly, he consistently pushed

Churchill to make concessions to Indian nationalist demands – in Roosevelt's view to make progress, in Churchill's view a form of defeat.

In February 1942, Roosevelt used his personal envoy in Britain, William Averell Harriman, to press Churchill about action on India. Roosevelt was alarmed by the report of the Chinese nationalist leader, Chiang Kai-Shek, who had toured India in February 1942, that the British were in effect 'presenting India to the enemy and inviting them to quickly occupy [it]'. Roosevelt warned Churchill that US soldiers in India would not assist the British to hang on to their empire even if an Indian uprising led to Japanese invasion and German and Japanese forces joining up in the Middle East to create a global occupation.

In response, Churchill blustered about morale in the Indian army and the danger of promises, but in March 1942 agreed that the war cabinet should announce that the lord privy seal, Sir Stafford Cripps, would be sent to India to discuss the implications of the declaration on dominion status made in August 1940.

The Cripps mission

Cripps travelled immediately to India and stayed throughout March meeting political representatives. His assessment was bleak:

> Unrest is growing amongst the population. The food situation is causing disquiet. The outlook so far as the internal situation goes is exceedingly bad.

Cripps had two parts to his brief: first, to explain and win backing for the August 1940 declaration by discussing the processes necessary to bring about dominion status; second, to discuss arrangements for the duration of the war on the basis of the 1935 Act with some minimal scope for additional Indian representatives on the executive council.

On 29 March he announced the conclusions of his discussions to a resounding lack of support, even from the British. Cripps returned to Britain on 12 April and offered his resignation. He was persuaded to withdraw it and Parliament debated his analysis of the mission's failure on 28 April.

Failure factors

Cripps himself identified the key factors as the war situation, including a defeatist attitude aggravated by enemy propaganda, together with Hindu–Muslim political antagonism. More generally, the government projected the view that its generous intentions had been repudiated out of hand. This rather simplified the complicated responses, intrigues and mistakes made by the various parties.

With regard to his first task, the postwar constitution, Cripps had stuck to the British government position that when a dominion constitution for a union of India was drawn up, provinces would be free not to join the union. Such protection of

Key question
What was the purpose of the Cripps mission?

Key date
Cripps mission: April 1942

Key question
Why did the Cripps mission fail?

this possibility at the outset was perceived by Congress as tantamount to encouraging Muslim disengagement from Congress and India itself. Indeed, at the press conference on 29 March 1942, Cripps discussed the possibility of two states, that is India and Pakistan, and even suggested altering provincial boundaries and the necessity of relocating masses of people. This was the first time a British official had publicly acknowledged this as a realistic consideration.

With regard to the second task, Cripps is criticised for going beyond his brief. It is suggested that, in trying to gain backing for the postwar processes, he was drawn into a proposal for an Indian defence minister on the executive council, which antagonised the viceroy, Linlithgow, and Churchill. The proposal was jointly made by Cripps and Colonel Louis Johnson, a personal envoy of the US president. Roosevelt had already proposed an immediate temporary dominion government on 10 March, saying:

> Such a move is in line with the world changes of the past half-century and the democratic processes of all who are fighting Nazism.

These interventions were perceived by the British as distrustful and meddlesome. They increased resistance if anything. Linlithgow already had Churchill's support because of his hard-line approach and the war cabinet backed Linlithgow's view that the powers of the viceroy were laid out in the 1935 Act and should not be tinkered with. In truth, the fact that Linlithgow had not been himself briefed about the Cripps mission virtually ensured that he and Cripps would be at loggerheads. This lends support to the view that Churchill had always regarded the mission as a way of placating the Americans and tarnishing the reputation of Cripps, who might be regarded as a political rival.

Congress rejection

Congress formally rejected the proposals on 10 April. There was little for them to support: the sole concession to them of the defence minister had been blocked, the princely states had been allowed to select rather than elect future representatives, while both the states and Muslims appeared to have gained the right to stay out of a future union of India completely. Moreover, Congress saw no point in rushing to agree if the deteriorating war situation would force the British to offer more later. Gandhi famously described the proposals as 'an undated cheque on a crashing bank'.

Although most observers saw Cripps as favouring Congress, the lack of engagement by Congress politicians again created opportunities for Muslims to bolster their position. The Muslim League was increasingly confident in challenging Congress' claim to represent all Indian opinion.

Churchill, Linlithgow and Amery all saw this as a helpful weakening of Congress and an excuse to postpone matters while there was such disagreement. Churchill maintained that the

British had done what they could and, indeed, US, Chinese and even Labour Party demands for progress diminished in the face of Congress' apparent ingratitude.

Quit India

The failure of the Cripps mission put negotiation over constitutional reform back in the drawer **for the duration**. Accordingly, both sides saw this as the opportunity to harden their approaches still further.

Linlithgow increased press censorship while using more centralised Special Branch surveillance to intercept Congress communications. He ordered a search for information to allow him to suggest that Congress was pro-Nazi.

Gandhi declared that Britain was unable to defend India but Indians should prepare a defence strategy of peaceful non-cooperation. He argued that, since Japan's hostility was directed at the British Empire, as soon as it was a free nation India would be able to negotiate peace with Japan. Congress declined to agree and Nehru, in particular, rejected any cooperation with a fascist power. In fact, Gandhi was ever more drawn to an unrealistic vision of ideal village life in a country withdrawn from the world. In his words: 'Leave India to God. If that is too much, then leave her to anarchy.'

By summer 1942, the government was aware through intercepts that a renewed campaign of civil disobedience was being planned. Linlithgow made plans to arrest the entire Congress leadership and deport them to Uganda while Gandhi would be sent to Aden. The plan was dropped when the governor of Aden objected and a lawyer pointed out that the power of arrest would lapse on board ship.

Nevertheless the war cabinet authorised Linlithgow to take all necessary measures after a further secret report revealed details of how the campaign would start with strikes and destruction of communications and railways. By now, the British government feared an uprising along the lines of the Easter Rising in Ireland in 1916, during the First World War, but on a massive scale.

The Quit India resolution

On 8 August 1942, the All-India Congress Committee met in Gowalia Tank park, Bombay, and resolved:

> to sanction, for the vindication of India's inalienable right to freedom and independence, the starting of a mass struggle on non-violent lines on the widest possible scale … every man and woman who is participating in the movement must function for himself or herself within the four corners of the general instructions issued.

Gandhi declared it the moment to 'Do or die for nothing less than freedom' and called bluntly for the British to 'Quit India', which became the popular reference for the resolution.

Key question
What effect did the failure of the Cripps mission have?

For the duration
Became a common phrase to describe the unknown length of the war.

Key term

Quit India resolution: 8 August 1942

Key date

British crackdown

Key question
How did the British respond?

Using a codeword, the viceroy ordered provincial governors to put into action prearranged plans for suppressing the civil disobedience campaign, overriding the opposition of the executive council. Congress leaders across India were arrested in morning raids. The Congress working committee was imprisoned in Ahmedanagar Fort near Bombay, but its members were allowed to meet freely and so continued political discussions. Gandhi was detained in the Aga Khan's palace at Poona (Pune) where he found that goats (to provide milk) had been positioned ready for his arrival.

Among the general population, matters were far less pleasant. The initial Delhi *hartal* resulted in arson and the killing of 14 people by police. The leader of the Congress Socialist Party planned to seize Delhi in a guerrilla war, calling on US soldiers to support them. Unrest, arson and sabotage grew in mostly Hindu areas such as Bihar, United Provinces, Bombay, Rajputana.

In response the police shot on sight those breaking curfew, and conducted public whippings; women were beaten with *lathis* and there were allegations of rape in custody. As violence escalated policemen were burned to death while the British burned whole villages and used aircraft to machine gun crowds. Hundreds were killed and about 500 arrested without trial and denied visits.

Emergency powers

In New Delhi, the Revolutionary Movement Ordinance was implemented, struck down by the courts and reissued with dismissively slight amendments by the government. Linlithgow was determined to crack down and was oblivious to the mounting evidence that maintaining British order was more important than the British rule of law.

Meanwhile, Churchill and Linlithgow were all but competing for self-importance and self-justification. Churchill declared defiantly:

> I have not become the King's First Minister in order to preside on the liquidation of the British Empire.

Privately, Linlithgow had already said:

> I do not think it is to exaggerate to affirm that the key to success in this war is now very largely in my hands.

Now he reported to the British government:

> I am engaged here in meeting by far the most serious rebellion since that of 1857, the gravity and extent of which we have so far concealed from the world for reasons of military security. Mob violence remains rampant over large tracts of the countryside.

Suppression

By the end of 1942, the British had managed to suppress the Quit India movement, using 57 infantry battalions to restore order. In the process, it was not only lives, liberties and homes which had been lost. The British had lost their moral authority within India and with American public opinion which once again saw the British as more interested in preserving their empire than defeating the common enemies of democracy.

Matters remained tense. The Indian members of the executive council all resigned while Gandhi declared from his palace-prison that he would undertake a three-week fast in February 1943. Even as his health declined, Churchill called him fake. Linlithgow announced that he would not submit to 'blackmail and terror' and made preparations to deal with Gandhi's death. As a result of personal pleas, Gandhi called off his fast in March.

But time was also being called on the Linlithgow era.

Key question
What was the effect of suppression on respect for the British?

Suppression of political campaigns: 1943

Key date

Public transport was a favourite target during the Quit India protests. To what extent might this be described as rioting?

| Summary diagram: Quit India campaign |

```
┌─────────────────────┐                    ┌─────────────────────┐
│   Cripps mission    │────────────────────│ Congress rejection  │
└─────────────────────┘                    └─────────────────────┘

                                           ┌─────────────────────┐
                                           │ Quit India resolution│
                               ┌───────────└─────────────────────┘
┌─────────────────────┐        │
│ Linlithgow crackdown│········ │
└─────────────────────┘        └───────────┌─────────────────────────┐
                                           │ Planned civil disobedience│
                                           └─────────────────────────┘
```

Key question
Why was Wavell chosen as the new viceroy?

3 | Viceroy Wavell

Churchill had twice extended Linlithgow's term of office, largely to maintain the suppression of the Quit India civil disobedience movement. Now that was under control, there was no good reason to postpone the choice of a new viceroy. Both Leo Amery, the secretary of state for India, and Clement Attlee, the Labour Party leader (and future prime minister), were considered. In the end, however, Churchill settled on a military figure, Archibald Wavell, the commander-in-chief of India.

The choice is revealing of Churchill's priorities. At first sight, it suggested the continuation of a hard line driven by military

Cartoon showing Viceroy Wavell's arrival in India. What relationship is suggested between the man and woman (princess) by the man's outfit? Who is controlling the elephant? How is Jinnah portrayed?

considerations. Another view is that confidence in Wavell had fallen and the 'promotion' to viceroy was a useful way of putting the more inspiring Auchinleck in his place as commander-in-chief. This would also suggest that political skills and experience were not sought in the viceroy, either because he would be closely controlled from Britain or because it was simply not recognised that political negotiation would be urgent and important.

Profile: Lord Wavell 1883–1950

1883	– Born in Colchester
1901	– Saw action in South Africa
1914–16	– Fought on the Western Front in France during the First World War
1941	– Allied commander of the south-west Pacific
1950	– Died

Archibald (Archie) Wavell was a career soldier and, at the start of the Second World War, commander-in-chief in the Middle East. He managed to defeat the Italian invasion of Egypt and Ethiopia but was later defeated by the Germans in North Africa. As allied commander in the south-west Pacific he was in command when Malaya and Burma fell to the Japanese. Up to this point the Allies had not secured any victories. However, Wavell had acquired something of the image of the wrong person at the wrong time. More objectively, he worked practically to end the Bengal famine and determinedly to make political progress despite procrastination in Britain. He has been described as 'a great man for solutions'.

Indian situation

Wavell took over an India which was paying vast sums towards the war effort. Britain was promising to repay afterwards but the total in 1943 was already £800 million, an amount that it was inconceivable Britain could actually repay.

Amery, commenting in his diary on Churchill's stated dislike of Indians, said:

> We are getting out of India far more than was ever thought possible and ... India herself is paying far more than was ever contemplated.

Wavell, having been based in India, came to the job better prepared than most viceroys. However, he came to London to meet political leaders. He soon realised that Churchill was paying lip service to the idea of political progress in India and that he had little awareness of the situation. He commented:

> He hates India and everything to do with it and as Amery said in a note he pushed across to me 'knows as much of the Indian problem as George III did of the American colonies'.

On returning to India, Wavell was told by Linlithgow that Britain would have to 'continue responsibility for India for at least another 30 years'.

Wavell became viceroy in October 1943 and, despite his experience, set about extending his knowledge and consultation. He travelled round the country, sometimes up to 1500 km per week, and convened regular meetings of the 11 provincial governors. (Linlithgow had not held one such meeting in his seven years.)

Wavell worked hard for India. His military training and lack of political experience proved useful in two key areas during his relatively short period of office. First, his response to a devastating famine in Bengal was practical and blunt. Second, he insisted on consideration of the details of the future boundaries of India and Pakistan in order to be prepared.

Key dates

Wavell appointed as viceroy: October 1943

Bengal famine: 1943–4

The Bengal famine

Key question
What was Wavell's attitude to the Bengal famine?

The situation in Bengal was critical. The two harvests of 1942 and 1943 had been low, the latter the worst of the century. This was aggravated by shortage of other foods and reduced imports because of the war and poor organisation of food distribution within the province. As a result of widespread malnutrition, people were dying more quickly of pneumonia, cholera and malaria. The death rate had risen by half as much again. In all, it is estimated that the famine itself caused between one and three million deaths.

Once the famine started to affect the major cities of Dacca and Calcutta, the concern became national (even international by assisting recruitment to the INA). It is much to Wavell's credit that he took a primarily humanitarian view that lives should be saved. However, he no doubt realised the political danger of doing little or nothing while trying to uphold the Churchillian view that British administration was good for India. Jinnah accused the British of incompetence and contempt on the grounds that such a crisis would not have been neglected in Britain itself.

Wavell's actions

Wavell immediately ordered military assistance for the distribution of food, in other words diverted soldiers from the war effort and defence of India. He introduced rationing and control of panic-buying and profiteering.

Politically, Wavell demanded the appointment of a governor for Bengal, a post which had been left vacant for no good reason. In Britain, he had to struggle against the view of Lord Cherwell, economic adviser to Churchill, that the famine was statistically improbable and with Churchill's own reluctance to spare any merchant ships to transport grain. Even the United States refused to divert any of its ships to Australia to bring in grain. However, Wavell eventually got twice what was originally promised, perhaps because it was half what he had asked for.

By mid-1944, the situation was coming under control but Wavell stated to Amery that

> The Bengal famine was one of the greatest disasters that has befallen any people under British rule and has done great damage to our reputation here.

Looking for initiative

Key question
What were the prospects for political progress?

It was also clear in the summer of 1944 that the war was being won. The D-day landings had successfully launched the Allied liberation of Europe, the Soviets were throwing the Germans back on the Eastern Front and the Americans were recapturing, with more difficulty, the Pacific islands. On the borders of India, the battles of Imphal and Kohima had decisively broken the threat of Japanese invasion. With military victory in sight, it was clear that pressure would resume for discussion of the postwar political situation.

In August 1944 Wavell brought the provincial governors together for a conference to consider the political future. Some new factors could be foreseen: the war debt continued to mount as would calls for repayment to benefit India and Indians; the Indian civil service had been strained by the war and hundreds of thousands of soldiers, both British and Indian, would be impatient to be demobbed and return home although there would not be enough employment to keep them busy.

The governors were 'emphatically of the opinion' that a positive initiative should be made by the British before the actual end of the war. The governor of Bengal proposed the unequivocal declaration of an actual departure date.

British attitudes

The problem was the attitude and interference of the British government and of Churchill, in particular. The government had raised the wages of Indian soldiers without consultation with the Indian government, adding more than £50 million per year to the war debt. On the other hand, Wavell's request for an Indian finance minister on the executive council was rejected. All Wavell's letters to Gandhi, in prison again in India, had to be sent to London first for discussion by the war cabinet.

Churchill simply wanted to do nothing. Far from concession, Churchill angrily declared that Britain was under 'no obligation to honour promises made at a time of difficulty'. While the war was on Churchill saw the importance of keeping up morale, although that did not hinder the suppression of the Quit India movement. With peace in sight, however, there was will neither to keep enough British soldiers in India to maintain order nor to supply money to create Indian forces. Indeed, ships and food were already being prioritised for the rebuilding of Europe.

Initiative stalled

In November 1944 Wavell requested consideration of a political initiative. For five months, the war cabinet put off responding and eventually left it to the India Committee to reject Wavell's request for any initiative. Wavell protested and was invited to London in March 1945 to make the case. He told Churchill that unrest was again growing and 'the present government of India cannot continue indefinitely or even for very long'. He declared:

> I feel very strongly that the future of India is the problem on which the British Commonwealth and the British reputation will stand or fall in the postwar period.

The trouble was that, while Churchill also saw it in terms of reputation, he was adamant that he would not go down in history as the prime minister who gave India away. Events would soon take that possibility away.

Wavell requested a summary of the India Committee's discussion in order to answer its concerns. The request was refused. The war cabinet stated that a precondition for progress was that Congress should officially declare the Quit India movement over. Wavell advised against stirring up what was already finished.

While Wavell was kept waiting in London for a decision, the economic adviser John Maynard Keynes presented the war cabinet with a financial analysis that showed that running the British Empire had cost £1000 million for each of the past two years, rising postwar to £1400 million per year. In sum, without US financial assistance, Britain would go bankrupt.

In the same month, April 1945, Roosevelt died. He had been a loyal but critical friend of the British when defeat had seemed possible. Now, a new president might not be so tolerant of British problems of their own making. Churchill's mind too was on managing victory parades with a view to the first general election in Britain since 1935. Almost as a way of getting Wavell out of his sight, Churchill agreed to a national conference of Indian political leaders. Wavell departed for India commenting that it was in effect too little too late yet again.

The 1945 Simla Conference

Wavell moved swiftly to make the conference happen. He released the Congress working committee from prison and ignored the rejection of the initiative by the executive council. The new members appointed because of Congress resignations could clearly see that their wartime support for the British would be swept aside by a resurgent nationalist movement.

The conference opened in the summer capital of Simla on 25 June 1945 with delegates from Congress, the Muslim League and others, both radical and loyalist. Wavell was exasperated by the assumption that votes around the table would be an acceptable way to make decisions about India's future.

The conference foundered quickly on refusals and rejections in creating a new Council, although Amery accepted that the delay in agreeing to even holding a conference had stoked up resentments.

Key date

Simla Conference:
25 June 1945

Jinnah (left) and Gandhi (right) during unsuccessful negotiations in 1944. What relationship does the body language seek to portray and reveal?

Jinnah refused to accept the legitimacy of Muslims who were not members of the Muslim League. The president of Congress was still Maulana Azad, still snubbed by Jinnah as a token Muslim in a Hindu organisation. Wavell had similar concerns about Congress, but he also refused to accept that the Muslim League was the only representative organisation of Muslims.

The governors of the Punjab and of Bengal advised Wavell to set out the consequences of creating a Pakistan in order to test the true strength of Jinnah's support in these two crucial provinces with their own local Muslim leaders.

Instead, Wavell proposed an Interim Council, with a membership list drawn up by himself. This was rejected by Jinnah, who sensed his growing popular strength with every refusal to compromise.

The conference broke up and shortly afterwards the political landscape was itself shattered. In July 1945, the British electorate voted unsentimentally to throw out Churchill, the great wartime leader, in favour of the socialist Attlee at the head of a Labour government committed to radical social reform. The omens for Indian nationalism had never looked better.

Nehru (left) and Jinnah (right) during the Simla Conference 1945. What do the different styles of dress suggest?

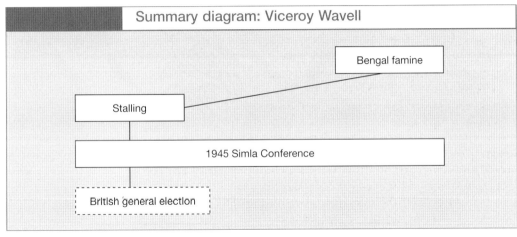

Summary diagram: Viceroy Wavell

Bengal famine

Stalling

1945 Simla Conference

British general election

Study Guide: AS Question

In the style of Edexcel

Source 1

From: Patrick French, Liberty or Death, *published in 1997.*

Events in East Asia during the early months of 1942 changed the complexion of Indian politics for good. In February the imperial fortress of Singapore surrendered to the Japanese without a shot being fired, through a combination of incompetence and poor planning, and the competing military demands of the war in Europe. It was a monumental blow to Britain's prestige in Asia, and led to the development of popular feeling in India that their British rulers were no longer invincible.

Source 2

From: a Japanese cartoon, published c.1942, urging Indians to throw off British rule. The caption reads 'All British colonies are awake. Why must Indians stay slaves? Seize this chance, rise!'

Source 3

From: Niall Ferguson, Empire, *published in 2003.*

Events in India [during the Second World War] revealed the weakness of the nationalist movement and the resilience of the Raj. The viceroy announced India's entry into the war without a word of consultation with the leaders of Congress. The 'Quit India' campaign launched in 1942 was snuffed out within six weeks by arresting Gandhi and the campaign's other leaders, censoring the press and reinforcing the police with troops. Congress split, with only a minority led by Bose choosing to side with the Japanese. And even his Indian National Army proved of little military value. It turned out that the only serious threat to the British in India were the Japanese divisions in Burma; and the Indian army defeated them at Imphal (March–June 1944).

Use Sources 1, 2 and 3 and your own knowledge.
Do you agree with the view that there was little change to British power in India during the Second World War?
Explain your answer, using Sources 1, 2 and 3 and your own knowledge. (40 marks)

Exam tips

The cross-references are intended to take you straight to the material that will help you to answer the question.

The following points can be found in the sources; how will you group them? What key phrases or, in the case of Source 2, what parts of the image, will you use to make these points? Where there is a chapter page reference, you can also add your own knowledge to develop or counter these points:

- The nationalist movement had weaknesses.
- British power was able to 'snuff out' the Quit India campaign quickly (pages 102–4).
- The Raj was resilient and able to withstand challenge (pages 103–10).
- Congress split.
- The surrender of Singapore to the Japanese was a huge blow to Britain's prestige.
- The surrender of Singapore encouraged a feeling in India that the British could be defeated.
- The Japanese attempted to incite the people of India to throw off British rule.
- Only a minority of Indians chose to side with the Japanese.
- Bose's Indian National Army was not a serious military threat (page 97).
- The Japanese forces in Burma were a threat to British power in India.
- The Indian army defeated Japanese divisions at Imphal (page 97).

From your own knowledge you can also include the following additional points. How will you organise them?

- The period of the Second World War marked a crucial change in Indo-British relations (pages 92–108); the influence of the USA encouraged sovereign rights and self-government in India (pages 99–100); the August 1940 statement offered postwar dominion status (page 95).
- But Winston Churchill was opposed to concessions to Indian nationalism (page 95); the failure of the Cripps mission (page 100) marked the end of negotiations for constitutional reform for the duration of the war (page 101).
- Wavell's view in 1944 was that the present form of government in India could not continue for long (page 109); the end of the war brought the realisation that British could not hang on to power in India much longer (pages 109 and 116).

What is your overall conclusion? The Japanese threat was defeated and no new constitution for India was put in place during the war. But had key changes which affected British power in India nevertheless taken place during the war?

5 Independence and Partition 1945–7

POINTS TO CONSIDER

The surprise election of a Labour government in Britain at the end of the war ensured that independence would be granted to India. A new, but final, viceroy, Lord Mountbatten, was appointed with instructions to accomplish this swiftly. However, relations between Congress and the Muslim League were breaking down so badly that this was not so easy to do. Communal violence increased relentlessly as the self-declared deadline approached for the British to depart. Although many had assumed that the borders between India and Pakistan were a formality, once independence arrived, it suddenly mattered enormously to people which side they were on, particularly in the divided Punjab. Terrible massacres took place among the hundreds of thousands trying to get across the border one way or another. The largest peacetime transfer of power in history ended in conflict and bloodshed amongst the winners.

This chapter examines in more detail:

- Negotiating positions around the demand for Pakistan
- British attempts to create plans for independence and partition
- Communal violence and partition massacres
- Resolution of the final relations with the independent princely rulers

Key dates

1945	May	British general election
	August 9	End of the Second World War
1946		Indian general election
	April	Cabinet mission
	May	Simla Conference
	May	Cabinet mission's May statement
	August 16	Direct action day
	September 2	Interim government took power
	December 7	Constituent assembly convened
1947	March 22	Mountbatten became last viceroy
	March	Congress accepted Pakistan demand
	May 3	Plan Balkan

	May 10	Mountbatten showed Nehru Plan Balkan at Simla
	June 3	Announcement of final plan for independence and partition
	July 4	Independence of India Act
	July 8	Territorial partition work began
	July 19	Interim government split
1948		Deaths of Gandhi and Jinnah
1950	January 26	India became a republic

1 | Options

The new Labour government voted into power in Britain in May 1945 was determined to press ahead with political reform in India and there was optimism among nationalist leaders that progress towards independence would quicken.

The two main aims were to revive democratic politics by holding elections for the 11 British provincial councils and the central assemblies and to form an (unelected) group to start work on a new constitution.

There was some concern among the British in India that the British government was not sufficiently aware of the scale of support for the Pakistan movement and that elections would provide a huge boost to the campaign. Nehru had said that he would not work with the Muslim League while Jinnah was strengthening the demand for Pakistan.

Key question
What were the aims and concerns of the Labour government in relation to India?

Key dates

British general election: May 1945

End of the Second World World: 9 August 1945

Fear of unrest

Viceroy Wavell was worried that Labour was too eager to hand over power to Congress, which would further raise the anxieties of the Muslim League. He was acutely aware of the potential for unrest – from food and coal shortages as much as anything – and the weakness of the British situation if the revival of politics led to renewed civil disobedience.

At the end of the war in August 1945 there were about 50,000 soldiers available in India (that is just one for every 8000 civilians) but, tired after the war, they were eager to be **demobilised** and return to their homes, whether Indian or British. It was inconceivable that extra troops would be sent. Moreover, any state of emergency would itself be more serious than ever before because of the widespread availability of unreturned weapons.

Wavell wrote to the new secretary of state for India, Freddie Pethick-Lawrence, in November 1945:

Demobilised
Released from the armed forces.

Key term

> We are now faced in India with a situation of great difficulty and danger … I must warn His Majesty's Government to be prepared for a serious attempt by the Congress, probably next spring, but quite possibly earlier to subvert by force the present administration in India … the choice will lie between capitulating to Congress and

accepting their demands and using all our resources to suppress the movement.

Courts martial and mutinies

The British did not help the situation by their handling of the defeated Indian National Army (INA). It became clear that Indians generally supported the captured soldiers. Congress called for their release, declaring:

> it would be a tragedy if these officers, men and women were punished for the offence of having laboured, however mistakenly, for the freedom of India.

The British officer class nevertheless still wanted to make the point that the INA were traitors and court-martialled a sample of three senior officers, deliberately choosing a Hindu, a Muslim and a Sikh. This simply united the three communities and their leaders in opposition. The officers were convicted of waging war against the Crown, a charge carrying a potential death penalty. They were actually sentenced to transportation for life, but then this was abandoned and they were released in case the general mood in the Indian army turned angry.

There were mutinies in February 1946 (and indeed there was unrest among British troops unhappy about the slow pace of demobilisation). A total of 20,000 sailors from the Royal Indian Navy in Bombay, then Calcutta and Karachi, took over nearly 80 ships and a general strike was called by the Bombay Communist Party. However, Congress leaders persuaded the mutineers to surrender. This angered many supporters but the leadership of both Congress and the Muslim League saw more advantage for the moment in cooperating with the British than in resistance.

Preparation for partition

It was apparent to nationalist leaders that the British were now serious about quitting India, which meant gauging the strength of the demand for Pakistan. In January 1946, a small fact-finding visit of British MPs came and went without announcing their conclusions, but in private some stated that Pakistan must be conceded to avoid Muslim unrest. In secret, work began on deciding how the country could be partitioned. Viceroy Wavell was keenly interested in making practical preparations for the eventual unpleasantness of announcing the actual boundary lines. It was immediately apparent that the Punjab would be a flashpoint split between a Muslim-west and Hindu-east but with five million Sikhs spread throughout. The Sikh holy city of Amritsar was surrounded by a Muslim-majority area, potentially cut off in a future Pakistan.

Meanwhile, British and Indian politicians were waiting to see how the land lay after the Indian general election in the spring of 1946.

Key date

Indian general election: spring 1946

Elections

The message of the election results in the 11 British provinces was even greater polarisation of support. In overall terms, Congress won a convincing victory with 90 per cent of seats. However, the Muslim League won 75 per cent of all Muslim votes, took 90 per cent of the seats reserved for Muslims in the provinces and all 30 Muslim seats in the central assembly. Congress was shocked to realise that it would have to face up to the Muslim League and their Pakistan campaign.

Congress formed provincial governments in eight provinces, the Muslim League formed two, in Bengal and Sind, while a non-Muslim coalition took power in Punjab, even though the Muslim League had the largest number of votes and took 75 of the 88 Muslim seats.

A more subtle message was that Muslims had voted most strongly for the League in Muslim-minority provinces that could never realistically be part of Pakistan. They appeared to support the idea of a separate Muslim state as a haven to which they might move. In the areas which were already Muslim-majority, there appeared to be more interest and confidence in maintaining local power.

In Bengal, for example, Huseyn Shaheed Suhrawardy, the local Muslim League leader, tried to form a regional coalition with Congress in order to campaign for a united, and possibly independent, Bengal. In Sind province, a breakaway group formed a minority government with the aim of an independent mini-Pakistan. In the North West Frontier Province, the Pathan tribes were not League supporters and Congress held power in this far-flung area beyond the Muslim belt.

> **Key question**
> What did the election results show?

The cabinet mission

In order to push forward with Labour's second aim – the drafting of a new constitution – Prime Minister Clement Attlee gained cabinet agreement for another mission to India. It was widely expected that this new peacetime mission, from a socialist government which clearly intended to honour promises of independence, ought to be successful. In fact, in the words of Woodrow Wyatt, a Labour MP:

> **Key question**
> How did the British prepare for a new constitution?

> they tried to give away an Empire but found their every suggestion for doing it frustrated by the intended recipients.

An official document of the time said that the formal brief was to consult about the:

> setting up of machinery whereby the forms under which India can realise her full independent status can be determined by Indians … with the minimum of disturbance and the maximum of speed.

The confidential brief was not just to listen but to create positive desire for a speedy transfer of power.

The mission, including 11 civil servants, was nominally headed by the secretary of state, Freddie Pethick-Lawrence, an ageing and genial socialist, but was driven by Stafford Cripps, now president of the board of trade in the cabinet, seeking to reverse the embarrassing failure of his 1942 mission. The third man was A.V. Alexander, First Lord of the Admiralty, but actually a very traditional Labour politician.

The mission met Indian politicians on 1 April 1946 and invited the various leaders to state their demands or aspirations.

Gandhi argued defiantly for power to be transferred to Congress, as the election winners, to make decisions about and for India.

Jinnah recognised that there was no hope of Pakistan from an independent Congress-dominated India. It could only come into existence from a British decision. The British needed Muslim cooperation in order to avoid disorder and present an agreed peaceful transfer to the world. So Jinnah avoided confrontation and waited. Gandhi made a wily suggestion that Jinnah form the government balanced by a Hindu majority in the central assembly, prompting Wavell to observe that 'he is a tough politician and not a saint'.

Meanwhile, there was no Sikh representative and little attention paid to this vulnerable minority. Similarly, the position of the princely states was ignored. They had treaties with Britain which

Illingworth cartoon. Who might the three humans represent? Why is the middle figure wearing a boy's sailor's outfit? Why are the others dressed as public schoolboys? What is the figure on the left holding? What does the cartoon predict for their future?

could not force them to become part of an independent India. In theory, they had the right to remain as autonomous petty states scattered across India.

The behaviour of the British delegation was counter-productive. Pethick-Lawrence wanted Indian independence so much that he left the British no bargaining power. He tended to agree with every demand, earning him the secret nickname Pathetic Lawrence. Cripps, meanwhile, enjoyed holding secret meetings but then made no secret of his closeness to Gandhi, attending prayer meetings and being sent daily yogurt.

The Simla Conference 1946

In May 1946, Indian political leaders were invited to Simla for a conference to discuss the two constitutional options drawn up by the cabinet mission and approved by the full British cabinet.

Wavell joined the three-man delegation to form the British party with four representatives each from Congress and the Muslim League. The mood was not good. Jinnah refused to speak to Maulana Azad, one of the two Muslim Congress representatives. Gandhi, although not formally involved, turned up on a special train to announce that he would block any moves towards partition.

The first, preferred option attempted to be imaginative and flexible. It proposed a single state with a three-tier constitutional structure:

- a minimal 'union government', responsible for foreign affairs, defence and communication
- self-selected regional *groupings* of provinces exercising all other governmental powers
- the existing provinces.

More controversially, it was proposed that the regional groupings might be permitted after a period of time to **secede** from the original union by means of **plebiscites** to become independent states.

The second, fall-back option was the first formal proposal of a two-state outcome: **Hindustan** and Pakistan. The two states would conclude formal treaties with each other but would have no common government.

The hope was that Congress would recoil from the second option and support the first. It had the attraction of producing a Congress-dominated single state but they would have to accept the right of provincial groupings to secede.

On the other side, although the Muslim League would obviously prefer the second option, they might be persuaded to accept the first if they were confident that sustained demand for Pakistan would allow it to emerge democratically.

The British cabinet was concerned about the viability of a Pakistani state in itself as well as the effect of splitting the Indian armed forces. There is, however, some evidence that the British regarded a future Pakistan as more loyal to British strategic interests in central Asia than a future India (see page 148).

Key question
Why did the cabinet mission plan fail?

Key date
Simla Conference: May 1946

Key terms

Secede
Peacefully break away from a state.

Plebiscite
A vote of the whole population on constitutional issues.

Hindustan
Literally the land beyond the Indus (coming from the west) – an Arab or Mughal perspective.

In the end, perhaps predictably, Congress could not give its support to either option since they could both lead, sooner or later, to partition. After two full sessions of the conference, with no prospect of agreement, Pethick Lawrence wound up proceedings.

With hindsight, historians have speculated about the role of the failing health of Jinnah. Jinnah's public stance of waiting until people came round to the idea of Pakistan was at odds with his personal fear that he did not have long to live. He wanted to see Pakistan born before he died and he wanted to be its first leader. He could not afford to wait another ten years or more for plebiscites to take place.

If Congress and the British had known how seriously ill he was, they might have been tempted to slow down and wait for him to die in the hope that the momentum would go out of the Pakistan movement. It is one of the great 'might have been' questions of the period.

The May statement

Key question
How did the British move on from the Simla failure?

Having failed to reach agreement in the Simla conferences, the cabinet mission moved matters on by making a declaration of intent, leaving it up to the various Indian parties to agree or not.

Key term

Constituent assembly
A parliament with the sole task of designing a constitution.

They announced that they would create a **constituent assembly** of elected representatives from the 11 British provinces. The assembly would draft a constitution for the single state with regional groupings.

Congress declined to accept the May statement. However, on 6 June, the Muslim League did accept it and Jinnah spoke publicly to emphasise the personal compromise he had made in accepting the right of a constituent assembly to decide about Pakistan.

Key date

Cabinet mission, May statement: May 1946

The cabinet mission further announced that it would create an interim government composed entirely of Indians, with the exception of Wavell as governor-general. However, this plan got stuck on the proportions of members for different communities. Jinnah insisted on choosing all the Muslim representatives, while Congress insisted on being able to choose Muslims for the Congress section. A Sikh and a Christian representative were added, followed by a Dalit and then a Parsi.

As time moved on, a further (June) statement announced that the viceroy would select members for any group which did not immediately accept the May statement.

Congress counter-interpretation

Key question
What were the political effects of upholding Congress' counter-interpretation?

On 24 June Congress suddenly announced a partial acceptance of the May statement. They were clearly seeking to avoid being excluded but they also proposed a counter-interpretation of the groupings plan. They argued that if groupings could secede from the nation-state, then individual provinces could opt out of regional groupings, either to become autonomous or merge back into the (Indian) state. Their hope was, of course, that this would fragment Pakistan if it ever got formed. To the anger of Wavell and Jinnah, Cripps declined to rule out this interpretation.

On 27 June, Jinnah, feeling betrayed, announced that constitutional methods had failed. The cabinet mission left India and Wavell wrote:

> The Mission gave away the weakness of our position and our bluff has been called. Our time in India is limited and our power to control events almost gone.

Wavell announced the imminent formation of the interim government on the basis of six Congress nominees, five from the Muslim League and three chosen by Wavell to represent minorities. When the Muslim League declined to nominate anyone, Wavell agreed that Congress should choose additional Muslim representatives.

The Muslim League responded by withdrawing its previous agreement to the May statement and instructed all Muslim officials to resign.

Withdrawal plans

As the political process broke down, so the country slid towards civil war. The commander-in-chief Auchinleck warned on 13 August that 'in the event of civil war, the Indian armed forces cannot be relied on'. Wavell was advised to 'leave India to her fate'. He wanted to announce a phased withdrawal which would be completed by 1 January 1947, just five months later.

However, the British government wanted no sense of panic so Wavell was refused troop reinforcements. He had almost been refused permission to even make plans for the evacuation of 100,000 European civilians, including many families, and only just got promises of extra ships if necessary.

Then, in the heat of August 1946, Jinnah made his first and last great misjudgement.

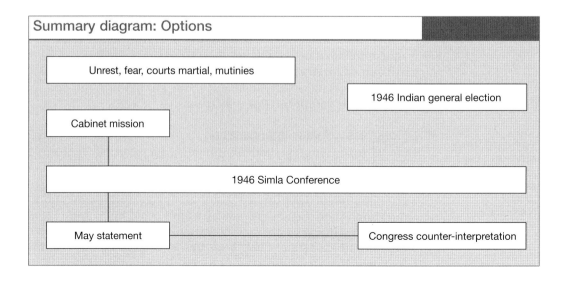

Summary diagram: Options

- Unrest, fear, courts martial, mutinies
- 1946 Indian general election
- Cabinet mission
- 1946 Simla Conference
- May statement
- Congress counter-interpretation

2 | Setbacks

The great Calcutta killings

Key question
Why did Jinnah resort to direct action?

Jinnah had decided that the time had come to show that the Muslim League could also use direct mass action like Gandhi and Congress. Jinnah had up to now deplored the use of such action, regarding it as a form of intimidation, and preferred entirely peaceful means of constitutional negotiation. However, he had now despaired of negotiations because of the tactics and behaviour of Congress leaders and was confident of a show of strength because of the election results. This combination of inexperience, confidence and despair perhaps led him to underestimate the forces he was about to unleash.

Key date
Direct action day: 16 August 1946

Jinnah called for a 'universal Muslim *hartal*' on 16 August 1946 which was declared direct action day. The symbolic focus of the strike was a huge Muslim League procession through Calcutta. Jinnah's intention was entirely peaceful and League leaders had persuaded the relatively new British governor of Bengal to declare a public holiday with the result that the army was withdrawn to barracks.

However, the tens of thousands of marching Muslims had provided themselves with *lathis* and rocks, for either self-defence or aggression. Hindus threw stones as they passed. At the final mass rally of 100,000 marchers, the chief minister of Bengal, H.S. Suhrawardy, is thought to have incited violence against local Hindus. As dark fell, the crowd moved off and the attacks began in the slums and the docks. There followed three days and nights of rioting, lynching, killing and arson before troops gained control again. Hundreds of bodies were left in the streets. The toll is now thought to have been 6000 people dead, nearly 20,000 wounded and 100,000 made homeless. Most of the latter moved to areas already strong in numbers of their religious community – a portent of the desperate migrations to come.

Causes and consequences

Key question
What were the political consequences of the Calcutta killings?

It was assumed that, since Muslims were responsible for the march, the vast majority of victims were Hindu. This is not now thought to be the case. Congress held the governor responsible for failing to prepare for rioting. However, elsewhere in India, the *hartal* caused no trouble at all. Commentators now believe that the initial trouble was exploited by the many underworld gangs of the vast, poor city of Calcutta, looking to settle scores and indulge in looting.

The outcome of the Calcutta massacres was the destruction of any optimism that the communities and their leaders might take political chances and offer compromises. The slope towards communal partition had tipped steeply. For Jinnah, it was a personal catastrophe. His reputation for wise leadership was damaged, whether one believed that he knew what he was doing or simply that the Muslim League could not manage its own community discipline.

Congress, notwithstanding its numerical strength, now felt the injured party and resorted to working outside and against negotiations. Gandhi warned Wavell that Congress would not try to calm any future trouble if that actually meant using British troops as back-up. Behind the scenes, Gandhi instructed the Congress representative in London to try to set up a secret meeting with the prime minister. Attlee agreed not only to the meeting but also to the suggestion that Wavell should be replaced as viceroy. Wavell got to know and, despite (false) reassurances from Attlee, it was clear that Congress was succeeding in undermining him.

The interim government

The long-awaited interim government took power on 2 September 1946, a moment described by the historian Patrick French as more important than independence nearly a year later. The 1935 Act had shifted power at the provincial level; now the balance of power at the national level shifted over to nationalist politicians.

Key date
Interim government took power:
2 September 1946

The viceroy was still responsible for the effective government of British India and relations with the princely states. However, as governor-general in council, the same person was now obliged to carry out the decisions of Indian ministers and members of executive council. Since the Muslim League had withdrawn its representatives, this meant that Congress was now in charge of India, including foreign affairs which were the personal responsibility of Nehru as vice-president of the executive council. Congress general secretary, Sardar Patel, was responsible for **home affairs**, which included security and the secret services. He immediately diverted the flow of intelligence reports to the Congress administration, cutting out the viceroy.

Key term
Home affairs
Government department for law, order and justice.

Wavell persevered with attempts to bring the Muslim League back into the interim government and in October they agreed to join the executive council. However, it was clear that it was not from a position of strength. The League did not have a veto over legislation concerning Muslims as it had previously demanded. Jinnah declined to join the executive council because of Nehru's dominance and appointed Liaquat Ali Khan in his place. When Wavell proposed the Muslim League be responsible for home affairs, Congress threatened to bring down the new government and Jinnah, avoiding a trial of strength, agreed to become finance minister.

To complicate matters still further, relations between Nehru and Patel had broken down since the elections for Congress president in April 1946. Patel had secured the votes of 12 of the 15 provincial Congress committees, but Gandhi made it clear he wanted Nehru and so it was decided. This was despite the growing distance between Gandhi's religious vision for independent India and Nehru's secular socialism.

Breakdown plan

Murderous consequences of the Calcutta killings spread throughout the final months of 1946. Muslims in Bihar province were killed in retaliation for the killing of Hindus in east Bengal who had themselves been killed in reprisal for the Calcutta violence. There was almost continuous rioting in Bengal, Bombay, Bihar and the United Provinces. The terror included forced conversions to Islam and forced marriages to Muslims. At Meerut, a police officer's wife was murdered with her eight children. Whole villages were destroyed and areas cleared of one community or the other. Twenty thousand Bihari Muslims died in 1947 with tens of thousands on the move.

In November, Wavell again warned the secretary of state, Pethick Lawrence, that the country was on the brink of civil war and asked for guidance. He had prepared a secret breakdown plan. In the event of the collapse of the interim government and law and order, all British civilians and families would be moved speedily to heavily protected safe zones near the coast in the north-east and west. They would be evacuated from Calcutta and Karachi. British troops would also be withdrawn leaving only Indian forces to maintain any order. Wavell, and the commander-in-chief, Auchinleck, agreed that:

> our present position in India is analogous to that of a military force compelled to withdraw in the face of greatly superior numbers.

Attlee refused to agree to the plan, saying that it would be accepting defeat. In fact, Attlee was stalling while he considered replacing Wavell, a situation which only let matters get worse.

The London talks

Eventually, Attlee agreed to summon Indian leaders to talks in London. Nehru, Jinnah, Liaquat Ali Khan and Balder Singh for the Sikhs engaged in four days of talks with Wavell and Attlee. The Muslim League was continuing to insist on the basic interpretation of the May statement, namely that groupings of provinces could secede from an independent India. On this basis, they saw no need for a further constituent assembly.

Constitutional experts agreed with this interpretation, but Attlee had taken against the Muslim League, describing Jinnah as 'an Indian fascist'. He reassured Nehru of his support for Congress. They would press ahead with the constituent assembly and Nehru flew back for its opening.

Jinnah remained at his residence in London, laid low by illness and disappointment. The 79 Muslim seats in the constituent assembly would be boycotted so there was no urgency to return.

Wavell too stayed on to press the case for a retreat plan. He also wanted decisions about the employment or pensions of the tens of thousands of British officials about to become unemployed upon independence. He made no progress. Indeed, his position was further weakened by the British appointment of a high commissioner to handle relations between the Indian interim government and the British Government, leaving the viceroy a figurehead.

Constituent assembly

The constituent assembly convened on 7 December 1946 but would never complete its task. Muslim demands for separate states grew ever stronger.

Constituent assembly met: 7 December 1946

Key date

Attlee was privately determined to force the issue by replacing Wavell with a new viceroy eager to hand over power as soon as possible.

In February 1947, Wavell was recalled to London and was told it was time for a change at the top. He was offered an earldom but no thanks for his work as viceroy. He was in effect sacked without dignity and everyone knew it. His view was that the Attlee government seemed as unclear what to do as Churchill's wartime government had been clear what not to do.

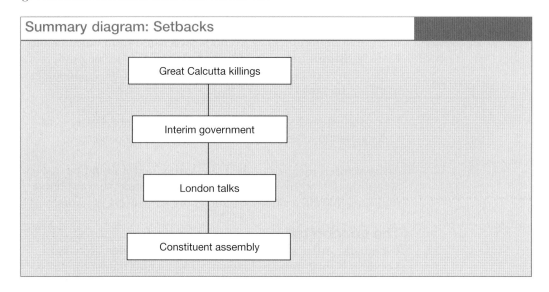

Summary diagram: Setbacks

Great Calcutta killings

Interim government

London talks

Constituent assembly

3 | Full Speed Ahead

The last viceroy

Attlee considered his choice of Lord Louis Mountbatten as the new viceroy to be brilliant. He was a military commander in the region and known privately to be sympathetic to the Labour government. He was moreover quite royal, being the king's cousin, which was appealing in a sentimental way since it was quite clear that he would be the last viceroy of the British Raj.

It is generally accepted that Mountbatten was full of self-importance, unjustified by his war record for example. Knowing that he had been selected for the position added to his desire to set conditions. He successfully demanded **plenipotentiary powers**.

Historian Stanley Wolpert takes an even more critical view, stating that Mountbatten knew the viceroyalty would be an interruption, however grand, to his naval career and he was

Plenipotentiary powers
The capacity to make decisions without approval from government.

Key term

Profile: Lord Mountbatten 1900–79

1900 – Born
1943 – Supreme Allied commander, South East Asia
1947 – Last viceroy of India
1947–8 – First governor-general of independent India
1979 – Died

Louis (Dickie) Mountbatten was born into a branch of the British royal family and was the great-uncle of Prince Charles. He served in the Royal Navy in the First and Second World Wars, during which he planned the disastrous Dieppe Raid. Before becoming viceroy he was supreme commander in South East Asia, based in Ceylon.

There has been much speculation about the relationships between the Mountbattens and Nehru. At the very least, there was a strong personal friendship between them all at the time. However, Lady Mountbatten is known to have had many previous affairs – a form of behaviour quite normal in British aristocratic marriages – and one which was known and tolerated by Mountbatten himself (perhaps because of similar, possibly bisexual, behaviour). For the rest of Nehru's life, Edwina visited Nehru and he stayed with her alone in England. It has been assumed that she developed an affair with Nehru: some say only later, others argue that it was an open secret since Jinnah resisted arguments to use it against Congress and the viceroy.

Lord Mountbatten was killed by the Irish Republican Army who exploded a bomb aboard his fishing yacht in Ireland in 1979.

determined to be brisk and brusque in handing India back. The fact that Attlee had replaced Pethick Lawrence as secretary of state by the young Earl of Listowel showed that no great experience would be applied to brake Mountbatten's impatience.

However, in contrast to the public display of power and self-confidence, Mountbatten also insisted privately on strict instructions from the Attlee government about political objectives. He wanted no setbacks to this final glorious viceroyalty.

The instructions Mountbatten received were to complete the transfer of power no later than the end of June 1948, having concluded a fair deal for the princely states and preserved the united strength of the Indian army. The public announcement of his appointment on 18 March included the objective of obtaining:

> a unitary government for British India and the Indian (princely) states, if possible within the British Commonwealth.

This latter point was Attlee's, and the king's, last main hope.

Mountbatten took over on 22 March. In later recollection, he claimed he was conscious of huge power. In reality, political events had a growing momentum of their own and Mountbatten needed to win approvals from politicians as before. In effect,

Key date

Mountbatten became last viceroy: 22 March 1947

Nehru (second from right) and the Mountbattens. What does the body language reveal about their relationship?

Mountbatten's role was to cover the feeble departure of the British in a little aristocratic glamour. Patel saw through it immediately and remarked that Mountbatten was a toy for Nehru to play with.

Mountbatten engaged in a series of meetings with political leaders while his wife, Lady Edwina, accompanied him in uniform on visits to troubled areas. Mountbatten was charmed by Congress politicians. Nehru with his English public school education was a favourite and was given time to be privately spiteful about Jinnah. Mountbatten admired Patel's bluntness but found Jinnah resistant to charm, judging him later to be 'a psychopathic case'. Dr Ambedkar insisted that Congress did not represent the 60 million Dalits or the three million Christians come to that.

Political stakes

The political stakes were higher than ever. The British wanted a peaceful handover under international scrutiny. The Muslims found Mountbatten much less sympathetic than Wavell, but knew that the best hope for Pakistan still lay with a British reluctance to simply walk away from a political disaster. For its part, the Congress leadership had come to the view that the first cabinet mission proposal – for a single federal state – would actually weaken the control of the national organisation.

Key dates

Congress accepted Pakistan demand: March 1947

Plan Balkan: 3 May 1947

Accordingly, and rather suddenly, in March 1947, Patel and Nehru persuaded the Congress working committee to accept publicly the demand for Pakistan (provided half the Punjab remained in India) in order to remove the point of compromising over a decentralised state. The Congress leadership had decided that even if Pakistan came into existence, it could not survive economically or politically and it would be reabsorbed back into a strongly centralised state of India. Such a victory would be worth both the gamble and the wait.

April conference

In April 1947 Mountbatten convened a conference of the 11 British provincial governors. They expressed grave concerns about the continuing growth of unrest and the likelihood of civil war given the increasing numbers of armed groups 'defending' the political parties. They recommended the earliest possible announcement of a definite plan for independence and partition if necessary.

However, it was also clear to all that no plan had a chance of peace without the agreement of Congress. Mountbatten thought that only a 'clean partition' would satisfy them. This would be no easy matter since Jinnah was now arguing that the two potential halves of Pakistan, East and West, should be linked by a land corridor, hundreds of miles in length cutting through Indian territory, but presumably under Pakistani control.

Key question
How did Plan Balkan envisage decision-making?

Plan Balkan

Mountbatten's first plan for an independent future was presented in secret to the British Cabinet on 3 May. It has become known as Plan Balkan after the European region renowned for splintered states almost continually at war.

The plan proposed that all decisions would be freely made at the provincial level. So, the 11 British provinces would be allowed to decide whether to be autonomous or join to form larger groups, not necessarily of comparable size. The provinces of Bengal and Punjab would be able to partition themselves if that was the popular preference. The princely states could also remain individually autonomous or join with others including former British provinces.

At best, this might be seen to permit or secure local agreement in the hope of a process of gradual formation of economically stronger groups. At worst, it seemed that Mountbatten was trying to wash his hands of any decision-making from the start. The cabinet was not impressed but made only minor amendments such as confirming that North West Frontier Province could become independent of a Pakistan swirling around it.

Mountbatten announced that he would reveal the plan at a conference of Indian leaders to be held before the end of May.

Meanwhile, Patel was calling for the immediate transfer of power to let Indians make their own plans whilst the most high-ranking Indian in the Army of India declared that a military dictatorship was probably the best course of action.

The Simla moment

Before the momentous announcement, Mountbatten took a private break with his wife at the viceregal summer residence in Simla. They were joined, at the viceroy's request, by Nehru and his daughter, Indira.

Whatever the truth about the personal relationships of the Mountbattens with Nehru, it certainly risked accusations of political favouritism to invite Nehru at this sensitive time. But perhaps Mountbatten planned to use social appearances to cover a political move which was clearly unfair and would have been indefensible if it had become public.

During the night of 10 May, Mountbatten showed Nehru the short document setting out his plan (Balkan) and asked him to give his response in the morning. Some consider this to have been a consequence of growing nervousness about the plan. Perhaps Mountbatten hoped that before the plan became public he could alter any matters likely to make Congress object. If that was his thought, he had a rude awakening.

Nehru sent him a confidential note on the morning of 11 May which slashed the plan. Nehru called it 'a picture of fragmentation, conflict and disorder' which would create a multitude of **Ulsters** all over the continent. Nehru blamed the British government for the impracticality and unacceptability of the plan, but that was perhaps to avoid embarrassing Mountbatten.

Nevertheless, one of Mountbatten's team said that not only was: 'British policy … once more in ruins but [Mountbatten] had endured a personal and most humiliating rebuff.'

Mountbatten asserted at a crisis meeting with his advisers on 11 May that the plan had only contained what Indians had previously indicated they would agree to and that his midnight tryst with Nehru had at any rate saved the day.

The Menon (June 3) Plan

In public, there was no immediate change to the intention of announcing the plan on 20 May. Behind the scenes, of course, an entirely new plan had to be decided and approved by the British cabinet. Moreover, by seeking Nehru's secret approval once, Mountbatten had effectively committed himself to ensuring his prior approval for any back-up plan.

With only hours before Nehru was due to leave Simla, V.P. Menon, the Indian reforms commissioner, was asked by Mountbatten to turn the dormant second cabinet mission plan into a credible document. This he did and Nehru pronounced himself satisfied. Rather incredibly, this two or three hours work became the basis for the greatest peacetime transfer of power in history.

Key question
Why did Mountbatten invite Nehru to Simla in 1947?

Key date
Mountbatten showed Nehru Plan Balkan at Simla: 10 May 1947

Key term
Ulster
Province in Ireland allowed to remain British.

The Menon Plan was for two states, India and Pakistan, with dominion status in what was now called the Commonwealth. Moreover, there would be no further deliberation by the constituent assembly as the states would use the existing political structures of the 1935 Act until they wished to alter them (in different ways). Provincial assemblies would decide which state to join, with the Bengal and Punjab assemblies also voting on the question of provincial partitions.

The princes would now decide whether to join not regional groupings but either India or Pakistan as states or, as before, insist on their autonomy.

Mountbatten informed the cabinet that the plan they had approved was now dead in the water but he had another. He was summoned to London with Menon and the original date for announcement of the plan passed.

Back in India at the end of May, Mountbatten embarked on a series of meetings to win groups over to the plan. He knew that Congress approved because they would easily gain control of a single Indian state, especially without the poor Muslim areas, and if dominion status was somewhat patronising, no one could stop them dropping it once the handover ceremonies had been forgotten.

Just to be sure, Mountbatten went to see Gandhi, who was not concerned enough to break his latest vow of silence, preferring to write comments on the backs of envelopes. For the Sikhs, Balder Singh, now defence minister, had literally no alternative and had to agree.

Jinnah, too, was finally in a corner. There would be a single, two-part, state of Pakistan but, with the almost inevitable partitions of Bengal and Punjab, it was no more than the area he had previously described as 'motheaten'. Moreover, the regional Muslim leaders were more than ready to do their own independence deals to secure their local power. This was finally the best deal he was going to get and within 24 hours Jinnah had given his agreement also.

Key date
Announcement of final plan for independence and partition: 3 June 1947

On the evening of 3 June, Mountbatten and the leaders went on All-India Radio to announce that a plan for the future of India and Pakistan had been agreed. The tone was hardly celebratory. The underlying message was that it was all that could now be rescued from the situation. Jinnah did attempt to end on a positive note with the phrase '*Pakistan Zindabad*' – 'Long Live Pakistan' – but with poor radio reception, it was heard as 'Pakistan's in the Bag' which sounded falsely triumphal and further antagonised Hindus.

Key question
How was the date for handover decided?

The precise date for the transfer of power appears to have been overlooked at first. According to the authors Collins and Lapierre, Mountbatten claimed to have been unprepared for the question at a press conference about the 3 June plan but improvised brilliantly in order to maintain his image of confidence. He instantly chose 15 August because it was the second anniversary of the Japanese surrender which ended the

Nehru, Ismay, Mountbatten and Jinnah (left to right) at the meeting to agree the final plan for independence and partition, 3 June 1947. What do the facial expressions suggest?

Second World War. With hindsight, this was perhaps not the date to mark the retreat of the British from India.

More significantly, it soon emerged that according to Hindu astrologers, 15 August 1947 was so horrendously inauspicious that a compromise had to be found. The transfer would take place at the stroke of midnight which might be regarded as the moment between the two days.

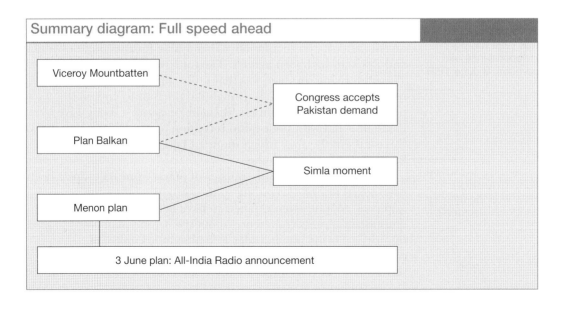

Summary diagram: Full speed ahead

- Viceroy Mountbatten
- Plan Balkan
- Menon plan
- Congress accepts Pakistan demand
- Simla moment
- 3 June plan: All-India Radio announcement

4 | Decisions

The Sikhs

The situation of the six million Sikhs was complicated and serious. Sikhs had dispersed across India (and the world), but were concentrated in the Punjab, where the city of Amritsar was holy to them. Relations between Sikhs and Muslims were never friendly. The prospect for the hundreds of thousands of Sikhs in the future Pakistan was not good.

The Sikh political party, the Panthic Pratinidhi, gained 22 seats in the Punjabi assembly in the 1946 elections and their leader, Tara Singh, claimed the right to autonomy. In fact, Jinnah offered autonomy within Pakistan but this was emphatically rejected. There was, however, no realistic prospect of a third, independent Sikh state.

During 1947, communal violence escalated in the Punjab, with Sikhs particularly fearful of the paramilitary Muslim guards. Tens of thousands of Sikhs began to move out of what would be Pakistan territory. The provincial government began to disintegrate.

The 3 June plan made no particular provision for the Sikhs despite promises of special consideration. Balder Singh was scorned for giving it his support. Local leaders spoke of uprising and civil war.

Rumours about the line of the eventual border raised tensions even more. In particular, the arrival of official army troops in the mainly Sikh district of Ferozepur meant that trouble was expected, which suggested it had been included in Pakistan, which in turn meant that Amritsar itself was at best surrounded by Muslim Pakistan or fully incorporated.

In fact, while this had been true for a while, the territory around Amritsar had been clearly marked for India but the troops had not been recalled. This one small area would be a flashpoint.

The princely states

Key question
What options were there for the princely states?

The legal position of the princely states was perhaps more complicated than the Sikh situation though hardly so dangerous. Strictly speaking, it was not even possible to talk of a collective position. Each of the 561 rulers had a separate treaty with the British, indeed a separate kind of treaty depending on whether they were union states, petty states, agencies or protectorates. With the departure of the British, each ruler was free to decide his own position. For a few states of a huge size and wealth continued independence was a tantalising possibility.

The British had no power to transfer a treaty even if the ruler wished it. Moreover, the nations of India and Pakistan did not yet exist and the princely states could not conclude new treaties with non-existent countries. So it looked unlikely that the transfer of power from the British to the Indian and Pakistani governments could also include a complete decision about the political map of the subcontinent.

In this light, it is remarkable that, in fact, hundreds of years of princely autonomy were abandoned so quickly and so easily. Two legal principles were key: paramountcy and accession.

Paramountcy

India had for hundreds of years been subject to a fluctuating mixture of foreign and regional powers. Nevertheless, there was no historical precedent for power to be relinquished or gained on a single day.

Congress seized the constitutional initiative and claimed that it should now be recognised as the paramount power and opened negotiations with the princely states in the future Indian territory. There was no objection: there were no realistically autonomous states in the future Pakistan territory and, it quickly transpired, the states themselves were ready to reach new arrangements.

Accession

In overall diplomatic terms, it was maintained that no decisions need be taken before 15 August. After that, the princely states would be able to conclude formal treaties with the constituted states of India and Pakistan. Out of diplomatic courtesy, it was maintained that such treaties might indeed recognise the independence of the princely state in question. However, states were welcome to **accede** to the new nations.

This courtesy actually permitted Congress, and Mountbatten, to work hard behind the scenes to push states to become part of India. Congress set up a states department to handle approaches to, and negotiations with, each of the rulers. For the time being, all criticism of the lack of democracy in the princely states was suspended.

Key term

Accession
The process of peacefully merging into a larger country.

Pressure

At the same time, all the small states without access to the sea were forced to confront their geographical weakness. Mountbatten assisted Congress by ruthlessly pressurising the rulers, publicly and privately. At a meeting of the chamber of princes on 25 July, he presented a scenario of constant fighting between local warlords with private armies, as in China. He wrote to each prince, telling them that his cousin, the king, would be personally insulted if they did not choose to become part of the new Dominion of India. He blithely promised that they would be free to become independent again if India became a republic, ignoring the fact that by then British promises would have no legal power.

This combination of Congress courtesy and royal arm-twisting resulted in a mass movement amongst the princes to accede to India. The princes would be allowed to stay as local rulers, with residual pomp and power to levy local taxes. India would be responsible for their defence and foreign relations and the territory would be officially part of India. As such, it has been calculated that Patel and Menon added more land to India than would be 'lost' by the creation of Pakistan.

The plan in reality

Earlier in the day of 3 June, the British had presented a dossier to Indian leaders entitled 'The Administrative Consequences of Partition'. Despite its bland title, it opened the final bitter and bloody phase of the independence struggle.

The dossier outlined matters for decision such as geographical boundaries, diplomatic representation, division of armed forces, civil departments, assets including railways, justice and the courts.

Decisions about decisions

The arguments started at the very next meeting over the prior question of who was responsible for making the decisions. Congress argued that it was for Indians to decide; Jinnah that it was for the British to decide how to dispose of their colonial property. He knew that the Muslims were unlikely to obtain as much from Congress as from the British. However, Mountbatten sided with Congress, arguing that the governor-general in council – that is he himself – was now executive officer of the Indian ministers of the interim government. Their decisions, ratified by the chief justice of India, would be final. Since Congress dominated the interim government, they would be Congress decisions and that, in effect, meant Sardar Patel decisions.

Congress forced confrontation of another issue. In their view, it was nonsense to think that India was being created. India existed and would continue. It was Pakistan which did not yet exist and therefore it was another nonsense to describe provinces joining a state which did not exist. They were seceding from India. Accordingly, if that was their choice they did not deserve any of India's assets.

Other attitudes

There was a considerable amount of desperately looking on the bright side: Mountbatten was told by an adviser that if he had not transferred power when he did, there would have been no power to transfer. Maulana Azad, the Congress Muslim leader, expressed a common view that:

> The division is only of the map of the country and not in the hearts of the people and I am sure it is going to be a short-lived partition.

There were also hardline attitudes: some Hindus were opposed to any partition even if voted for by provincial governments and some Muslims demanded that the historic Muslim capital of Delhi be part of Pakistan whatever the local wish (likely to be for India).

Provincial decisions

As set out in the 3 June plan, assemblies of the affected provinces held votes to determine which of the future states they would join:

- Sind and Baluchistan voted with straightforward majorities for being part of a Pakistani state.

- In the complex communal provinces of Bengal and Punjab, Muslim representatives voted for undivided provinces to be in Pakistan, whereas the Hindu and (Punjabi) Sikh representatives voted for partition so that their majority areas might be in India. The provinces would accordingly be divided.
- In the North West Frontier Province, a full plebiscite was held because it was recognised that there was considerable support for Congress or even the creation of a separate tribal area: 'Pakhtunistan'. The Muslim majority decision was to be part of Pakistan.

The Independence Act

With these decisions, the way was open to frame the independence bill, which would create the two new states. This was done in a matter of days, even including securing the agreement of both Congress and the Muslim League to the wording in advance of parliamentary discussion. On 3 July, the India committee of the British government worked until midnight to finalise the bill which was printed during the night and presented to the House of Commons on the morning of 4 July. It was passed immediately without amendment let alone objection (and one in a bunch of bills) and became law in mid-July.

Key dates

Independence of India Act: 4 July 1947

Interim government split: 19 July 1947

Assets and the partition council

A dedicated partition council was set up in June 1947 to reach decisions on the division of the assets currently belonging to the British in India. Every item, from steam locomotives down to typewriters, had to be apportioned. More acutely, every single administrator and civil servant would have to choose or be deployed to one new country or the other.

Key question
How were assets apportioned?

On the partition council, Sardar Patel and Rajandra Prasad represented Congress; Liaquat Ali Khan and Abdur Rab Nishtar, soon replaced by Jinnah himself, the Muslim League.

The partition council became in effect the government of (British) India because there was no other more important business now than deciding this division. (The geographical division was out of Indian hands.) On 19 July the interim government formally split into two interim governments, one for each of the imminent states.

However, behind the public façade of two new, constitutionally equal, states, Congress exerted maximum control on the basis that Pakistan was seceding and forfeited any right to Indian property. Similarly, any official who selected employment in the future Pakistan was immediately ejected from their workplace. The planning for Pakistan was undertaken in tent offices with scarcely any equipment.

For this reason, Liaquat Ali Khan wanted partition, if not actual independence, brought forward two weeks to 1 August. This attitude runs counter to the argument that Mountbatten should be held responsible for the rush to independence and partition. However, there is no escaping the shameful partisanship he displayed over the decisions of future pomp and ceremony.

Governor-general

India and Pakistan were to become separate dominions within the Commonwealth. As such, they would retain the British monarch as head of state, with a constitutional and legislative structure like Britain of the crown-in-parliament. They would retain a governor-general to represent the Crown element in their own territories.

Mountbatten had assumed that he would become governor-general of both the successor states. He considered this would show proper care and impartiality. This was despite his evident antipathy to Jinnah, the Muslim League and Pakistan, and his lack of concern about their treatment by Congress in the partition council decisions.

Jinnah wrong-footed him with a radical but rational decision. He declared that there was no need for a British governor-general and that he would bear the responsibility himself. It was clear to the Muslims that a weak Pakistan would only come under more pressure from having the same governor-general as a strong, hostile India. Mountbatten now found himself at the receiving end of the same *realpolitik* that he had supported when it was Congress exerting the control and pressure. He was faced with the choice of resigning, impartially, on independence day or revealing his favoured relationship with India. He chose to keep the governor-generalship of India (which actually had to be offered first by Nehru on 15 August).

Mountbatten was also forced to acquiesce when Jinnah pointed out that George **R.I.**, the king's official title, would no longer be acceptable in Pakistan since the 'I' clearly had no further basis in constitutional reality.

Border decisions

As early as February 1946, Viceroy Wavell had defined a specific line of demarcation between future Indian and Pakistani territory (on a map, not in reality). No further work was done until the

Key terms

Realpolitik
A term for political leverage, borrowed from the German language.

R.I.
Rex Imperator, Latin for King-Emperor.

Key question
How were the borders decided?

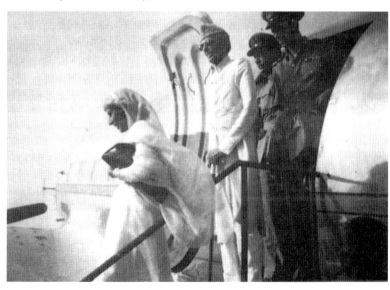

Jinnah arrives in Pakistan on 7 August 1947 with his sister Fatima. Compare his clothing with the photograph of Nehru and Jinnah on page 111.

partition council commissioned an independent British lawyer to draw up proposals. Sir Cyril Radcliffe KC (King's Counsel) arrived in New Delhi on 8 July, 36 days before independence, and hid himself away in order to create an air of neutral consideration of maps and statistics, rather than listening to political arguments.

Two separate boundary commissions were established, one for the border between West Pakistan and India and one for the border around East Pakistan. The former involved the partition of the Punjab, the latter the partition of Bengal. Each commission had two Muslim and two non-Muslim high court judges with Radcliffe as chairperson to exercise the decisive casting vote in the event of split decisions.

Territorial partition work began: 8 July 1947

Key date

Criteria

The commissions used census data to identify the majority community in each **district** of the relevant provinces along the provisional demarcation line. They then tried to ensure that the districts of a particular majority could be grouped so as not to leave any district surrounded by a different communal majority. Every district should be **contiguous** at some point with a district of the same majority.

It was recognised that the 1941 census would be out of date and might be seriously wrong in the case of the Punjab, in particular, since many Sikhs had been away in the army at the time.

District
A formal subdivision of a province.

Contiguous
A formal term for touching or adjoining.

Cartographical
Relating to maps.

Key terms

Assumptions

Various assumptions surrounded the issue of boundaries. These were never really dispelled because what emerged was never actually publicised for discussion. It was simply announced by the British as a fact.

In the first place, Jinnah had from the start of the Pakistan demand been careful not to get involved in discussions about actual borders. Nothing was done to dispel hopes of a so-called 'greater Pakistan', including undivided provinces of Punjab and Bengal and perhaps even reaching Delhi in the east. It was on the basis of this unconfirmed idea that the elections of 1946 had taken place.

There was a Congress assumption, as previously noted, that Pakistan could be 'given away' because it would fairly quickly come to its senses and be reintegrated.

The most widespread assumption was that the borders would be largely theoretical or **cartographical**. It was assumed that in practice, people would come and go across the border freely. The precise line might appear to cut villages off from their fields, for example, but farmers would simply live in one country and work in another a few hundred metres away. Certainly, middle-class Muslims, such as Jinnah, intended to keep homes in India as well as Pakistan and travel frequently between them. On this assumption, it was felt even in June 1947 that independence might arrive without confirmed decisions which could all be worked out in due course.

In the end, Mountbatten did indeed postpone the announcement of the frontiers until after the independence ceremonies. Although he claimed to have no knowledge of the details, he had realised that there would be trouble which would quickly take the joy out of the celebrations.

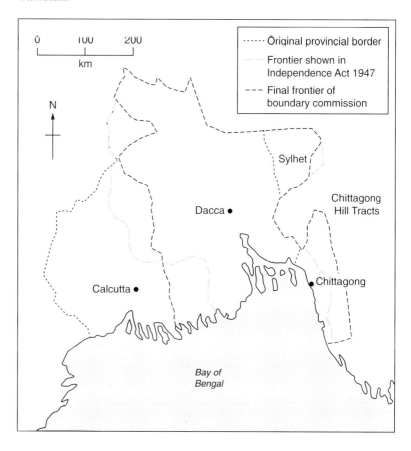

Problems

The borders determined by Radcliffe were basically the same as those secretly drawn up by Wavell in 1946. The unexpected and tragic reactions created by their notification will be dealt with in the next section. A number of other matters may be noted here.

On the eastern edge of East Pakistan, a tribal area called the Chittagong Hill Tracts, which was neither Muslim nor Hindu, was awarded to Pakistan. The main reason appears to have been to include the port of Chittagong within East Pakistan which was not going to include the great Bengal port of Calcutta. Indeed, to create an Indian zone around Calcutta a small Muslim area to its north was awarded to India.

In the Punjab, the key problem was that Amritsar district, containing the holy city of the Sikhs, was largely surrounded by Muslim-majority districts. In addition, for a while, even Ferozepur district, despite being a Sikh-majority area, had been marked for Pakistan.

Key question
Why did the border line become a flashpoint?

0   100   200
km

N

Original provincial border

Frontier shown in Independence Act 1947

Final frontier of boundary commission

Sylhet

Chittagong Hill Tracts

Dacca •

Calcutta •

• Chittagong

Bay of Bengal

Partition of Bengal in 1947.

It was decided to award a small portion of Lahore district to India, even though Lahore city itself was to be in Pakistan. In addition, the Gurdaspur and Ferozepur districts were placed on the India side of the line.

However, additional troops had already been sent to Ferozepur district in anticipation of trouble. The plans were changed but this was of course unknown to the local population who were alarmed by the arrival of the troops. The alarm would escalate throughout the province and lead to terrible massacres.

There is confusion and controversy to this day about this small but tragic detail of partition. Radcliffe destroyed all his notes on completion of his task so his reasoning is not known. French argues that the original allocation of Ferozepur to Pakistan was in order to ensure that the headwaters of the Sutlej river were protected from diversion into Indian Punjab irrigation. Wolpert argues that Gurdaspur was reallocated to India to protect the last Indian strategic road route up to Kashmir. This princely state had not yet decided its future but the later revelation of this change has led many to see a plan to force Kashmir to accede to India (see page 146).

One other area of dispute was the Andaman Islands lying off Burma. During the war, these islands had been given to the Indian National Army by the invading Japanese. Now Congress claimed them for India. The Muslim League argued that if there was to be no land connection between the two halves of Pakistan, then they should be granted the islands as a refuelling base. The British also wanted them as a strategic base in the Indian Ocean since they were about to lose the entire subcontinent and all its naval dockyards.

Independence arrives

At the stroke of midnight between 14 and 15 August 1947, the British Raj came to an end and the two nations of India and Pakistan came into existence.

Other imperial matters

The remaining French colonial possessions in India – mainly coastal cities including primarily Pondicherry – were not absorbed into India until 1954.

Portugal, under the Salazar dictatorship, refused to negotiate over its colonial cities, including Goa. They were eventually invaded and annexed by India in 1961.

Burma, which had become a separate territory of the British Empire in 1937 as a provision of the 1935 Government of India Act, became independent in 1948 and was later named Myanmar.

Ceylon, not actually part of British India although part of the Empire, became independent in 1948 and was renamed Sri Lanka.

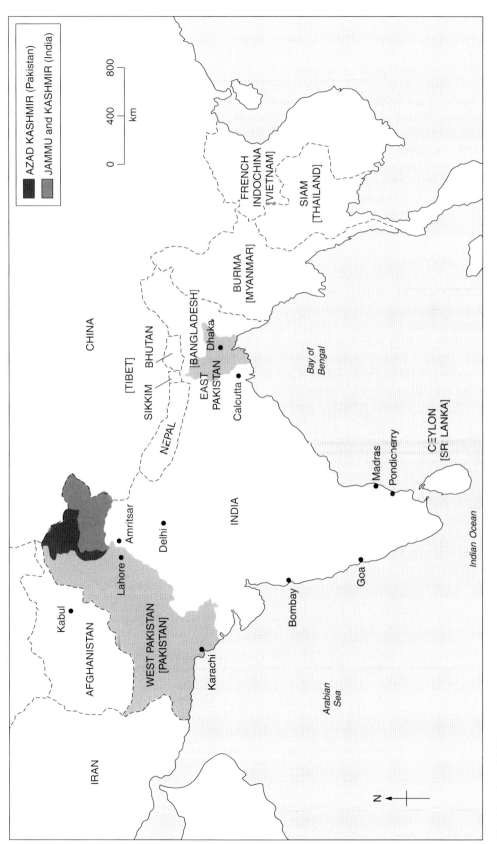

Legend:
- AZAD KASHMIR (Pakistan)
- JAMMU and KASHMIR (India)

Scale: 0 — 400 — 800 km

CHINA

[TIBET]

SIKKIM

BHUTAN

[BANGLADESH]

NEPAL

EAST PAKISTAN

Dhaka

Calcutta

Bay of Bengal

BURMA [MYANMAR]

FRENCH INDOCHINA [VIETNAM]

SIAM [THAILAND]

IRAN

AFGHANISTAN

Kabul

Lahore

Amritsar

Delhi

WEST PAKISTAN [PAKISTAN]

Karachi

INDIA

Bombay

Goa

Madras

Pondicherry

CEYLON [SRI LANKA]

Arabian Sea

Indian Ocean

N

Final borders 1947.

Mountbatten had attended ceremonies with Jinnah in Karachi on 14 August but was firmly back in India by evening.

Nehru went on All-India Radio to make one of the most poetic, apparently unscripted, political speeches in history. He declared:

> Long years ago we made a tryst with destiny and now the time comes when we shall redeem our pledge, not wholly or in full measure, but very substantially. At the stroke of the midnight hour, while the world sleeps, India will awake to life and freedom. A moment comes which comes but rarely in history, when we step out from the old to the new, when an age ends, and when the soul of a nation long suppressed finds utterance … This is no time for ill-will or blaming others. We have to build the noble mansion of free India where all her children may dwell.

Radcliffe departs

Radcliffe left India on 17 August as the border decisions were announced. There was widespread condemnation. As the scale of the human consequences became apparent to the world, the newly formed United Nations launched an inquiry. Radcliffe argued that he could not be held personally responsible for the aftermath. His task had been to make recommendations to the viceroy whose responsibility it was to reject them or accept and announce them. Radcliffe was so appalled at being made the scapegoat that he refused to accept payment for the job done.

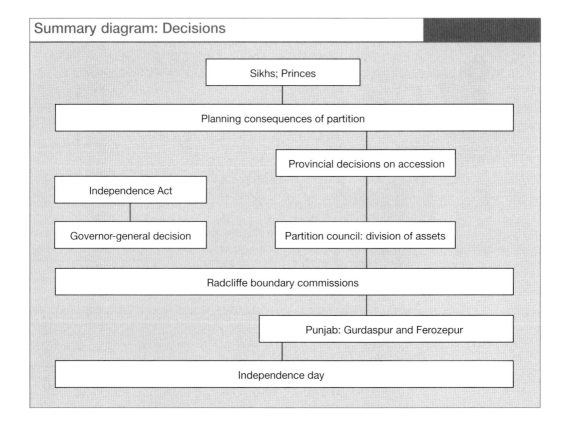

Summary diagram: Decisions

Sikhs; Princes

Planning consequences of partition

Provincial decisions on accession

Independence Act

Governor-general decision

Partition council: division of assets

Radcliffe boundary commissions

Punjab: Gurdaspur and Ferozepur

Independence day

5 | Aftermath

Migrations and massacres

Mountbatten and Supreme Commander Auchinleck had agreed that the priority for remaining British troops was to protect an early withdrawal of Europeans from the subcontinent. Accordingly, Auchinleck began the process of recalling troops on 15 August. However, there was no violence directed at British troops or civilians during the departure phase. It quickly became clear that fear, anger and revenge would be intensely communal. It is debatable whether both of these factors were because the secretary of state, Listowel, made a statement that troops would not intervene in any communal disturbances after independence. The broken Indian and Pakistan armies were not in a position to immediately take up maintenance of order.

As a consequence, armed militias arose to protect and to intimidate. In the Punjab, Sikhs organised into **jathas** of about 30 men operating outside the law and across borders as they thought necessary. A semi-formal, multi-religious Punjab boundary force, about 20,000 strong, came together but could not protect over 17,000 villages.

On 14 August, 38 Sikhs at Lahore train station, waiting to travel out of what was about to become part of Pakistan, were knifed to death. Later the same day, a Muslim mob set fire to a **gurdwara** in Lahore burning to death hundreds of Sikhs gathered inside for protection.

The next day, independence day, Muslim women in the Indian Punjab were dragged into the streets, stripped, raped and hacked to death.

On 20 August, militiamen of the Punjab boundary force shot dead 84 participants in a Muslim mob. On 24 August, Muslim members of the force were killed by their fellow Hindu soldiers, after having shot Hindu looters. The force split along communal lines and on 1 September was broken up completely. There was no law and order in the Punjab for weeks on end.

Massacres

Massacres of whole villages began. Thousands were killed every day. As fear and panic spread, hundreds of thousands, even millions, of people left their homes to attempt to reach the relative safety of the other country of their co-religionists. As they walked in endless lines, they were even more vulnerable to attack.

Most memorably infamous are the trains pulling into their destinations without a living passenger, the thousands of refugees aboard having been massacred and sent on their way. A reporter for *The Times* watched a train full of 4000 Muslims being carefully shunted into a station siding in preparation for a cold-blooded massacre. Eventually, trains started running again with armed guards.

Criminal gangs preyed on migrants, death squads worked through lists of names to clear neighbourhoods. Victims were

Key terms

Jatha
A squad.

Gurdwara
Sikh temple.

publicly humiliated, tortured and genitally mutilated before being killed.

As law and order disintegrated and thousands of bodies were left to rot in the August heat, cholera and other diseases spread rapidly, causing more fear and flight. It is said that the vultures were too fat to fly.

Mass rape

Mass rape was used as a weapon of war. Hindu, Sikh and Muslim women alike committed suicide when surrounded, often by throwing themselves down wellshafts. In some cases, men killed their families rather than let the mobs get to them. Women and girls were also abducted, forcibly converted and 'married'. Even when located in later years, the women were afraid to return to their own communities because of what they had been forced into.

The personal and financial strain of the refugee crisis was intolerable. More than half a million refugees arrived in Indian Punjab, making the province bankrupt. Hundreds of thousands struggled on to Delhi, barely surviving in squalid camps where women and girls were sold in exchange for food.

Death toll

All the authorities publicly underestimated the death toll. The British preferred it to be seen as continuing unrest but on a larger scale; they did not want to be accused of causing, and then

Cartoon about the aftermath of partition. What do the various central figures represent? What is their reaction to the events around them?

turning their back on, an unprecedented human catastrophe. The Indian and Pakistani governments quite simply wanted to avoid inflaming the situation or appearing incompetent. At the time, it was said that 200,000 died; a figure of about a million is now regarded as more accurate.

The massacres have left a psychological scar across the political act of partition and the birth of the two independent nations. In the Punjab, it was nothing less than civil war, and in the opinion of some, communal genocide. The dubious current term of 'ethnic cleansing' would certainly be applied: less than 1 per cent of the population of Pakistani Punjab is Hindu or Sikh and less than 1 per cent of the Indian Punjab population is Muslim.

The princely states

On independence, India and Pakistan were able to conclude legal treaties with the princely states. Within two years, as a result of the determined negotiations of Menon and Patel, all but three of the 561 states had acceded to what was termed the Indian Union. Only three States resisted: Junagadh, Hyderabad and Kashmir.

Junagadh

The Nawab of Junagadh, a small coastal state in the north-west, had opted to accede to Pakistan on independence even though

Refugee train in the Punjab in 1947. What would be the advantages and risks of escaping by train?

the two were separated by 300 miles of Indian territory. Mountbatten had not argued against this plan when he was still viceroy. Patel had other ideas. He ordered the Indian army to blockade the state, threatening mass starvation. The Nawab fled by sea to Pakistan, the army 'invaded' and a quick plebiscite resulted in an overwhelming popular vote to join the Indian union.

Hyderabad

The Nizam of Hyderabad declined to join either India or Pakistan on the principle that modern nation-states should not be formed for religious reasons. Although landlocked in the centre of the subcontinent, he could afford this high-minded stance because Hyderabad covered tens of thousands of square metres (larger than many members of the United Nations), had its own army and the Nizam was then the richest man in the world. He was able to lend the new Pakistan government 200 million rupees without hesitation. It was agreed that there should be a one year 'standstill agreement'. After the departure of Mountbatten (in 1948), Nehru and Patel ordered the annexation of the state, the army invaded (really invaded this time, since the ruler resisted) and after four days of fighting, the Nizam gave in.

Kashmir

The problem of Kashmir has still not been resolved. Kashmir was a large, mixed princely state right up against the mountains of the Hindu Kush and the Himalaya where the Indus river of Pakistan begins. The population was 80 per cent Muslim but was ruled by a Hindu Maharajah, Hari Singh, from his court at Srinagar. However, the Muslims were of a different (Sufi) tradition to the Muslims of the Punjab, now Pakistan. In addition, there was a considerable Buddhist population in the Ladakh area.

Kashmir adjoined the Punjab and if that had become wholly Pakistani there would have been no border with India. The partition of the Punjab resulted in some contiguity with the post-independence province of Himachal Pradesh but only through mountainous territory. Most land routes into upper Kashmir were through Pakistani territory, except one, through the controversial Gurdaspur district.

It made a lot of sense, both demographically and geographically, for Kashmir to join Pakistan. The Maharajah for his part seems to have thought that the British would never actually leave, forcing him to choose. When it came to pass, he attempted to model the state's future on Switzerland's neutrality. When that failed, he opted for India: some say because he feared that Kashmir would suffer communal violence as had Punjab and Bengal; some say his family feared to live in an Islamic state.

Provocations

The events in Kashmir of 1947–8 are controversial to this day and subject to nationalist interpretations. According to the Indian version, Hari Singh tried to secure a standstill agreement as in

Key question
Why did the region of Kashmir cause particular problems for settling the borders of India and Pakistan?

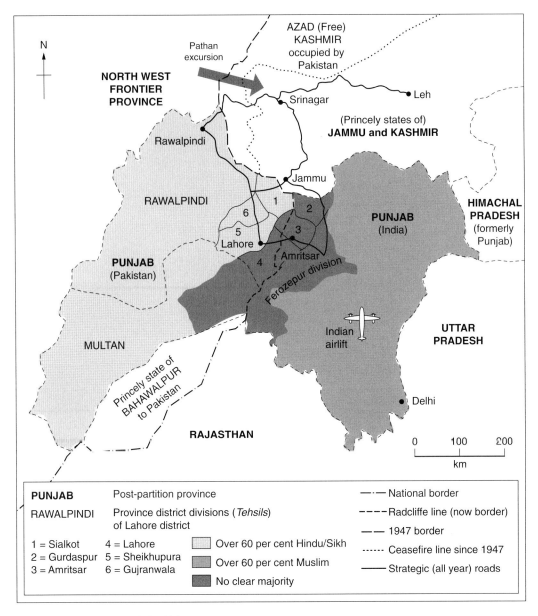

The Punjab and Kashmir in 1947.

Hyderabad, to which Pakistan agreed but India did not. Pakistan then applied economic pressure for a decision by restricting supplies along the roads in Pakistani territory. On the night of 21/22 October 1947, Pathan irregular troops, led by Pakistani officers, entered Kashmir and proceeded towards Srinagar. The border areas of which they took control are still occupied by Pakistani troops and are marked on maps as Azad (Free) Kashmir.

According to the Pakistani version, Kashmiri troops had been harassing Muslims out of Kashmiri villages along the border with Pakistan in order to create a depopulated zone which was easier to protect. It was this harassment which provoked the Pathans to come to their support.

Divergent motives

From this point, there also appear to be divergences in British and Indian motives.

Hari Singh appealed for Indian military assistance which Patel was prepared to organise. Nehru, whose family originally came from Kashmir, is often thought to have secretly arranged for Kashmir to become Indian. In fact, he repeatedly blocked Singh's request on a matter of democratic principle.

One popular Muslim leader in Kashmir, Sheikh Abdullah, had been imprisoned by the Maharajah. Nehru demanded that Singh release Abdullah and hold a plebiscite to determine transparently the wishes of the people. Nehru was prepared to accept that the overall vote might be for Pakistan. He also argued that if it was for India then whatever land the Pathans had occupied could be retaken. Singh refused to release Abdullah.

Mountbatten, now governor-general of India, sided with Patel's wish to intervene on the narrow legal grounds that princes were free to decide the fate of their states without plebiscites. However, he would not agree to military assistance until Hari Singh had signed the accession document.

It now appears to some historians that the British government, as distinct from Mountbatten, really wanted Kashmir to belong to Pakistan. Kashmir was the most northerly area of the former Raj. Britain retained a strategic interest, supported by the USA, in monitoring Soviet and Chinese activity across the border. Britain trusted Muslim Pakistan more than an India governed by Nehru who openly supported the Soviet Union and Communist China. Attlee repeatedly refused to support Mountbatten's hasty actions in support of India.

Memoirs of Pakistani generals have revealed that a further strategic interest was the major road running along the Pakistani side of the border between Lahore and the army headquarters at Rawalpindi. An Indian Kashmir could allow India to invade and cut off troop reinforcements to the Punjab in a matter of hours.

Two matters remain confused.

The accession document

First, the records show a flurry of plane flights between Delhi and Srinagar culminating apparently in a signed accession document, accompanied by a promise from Hari Singh to Nehru that he would release Abdullah and hold a plebiscite. The United Nations has repeatedly called for this plebiscite to be held but India refuses to organise it until Pakistani troops withdraw from Azad Kashmir.

Indian troops were airlifted into Srinagar, saved the Maharaja and held the Pathans back. Whether the airlift started before the accession was actually signed remains a question. There seems reason to believe that Patel pulled the wool over Nehru's eyes for a crucial few hours and days.

The accession was certainly claimed as the reason why the (British) commander-in-chief of the Pakistan army refused to commit Pakistani troops when the Indian army entered Kashmir.

The Gurdaspur district

Second, it was recalled that the Punjabi Muslim-majority district of Gurdaspur was actually put on the Indian side of the border. The official reason was to ensure that Amritsar was not surrounded by Pakistani territory.

The Kashmir crisis led to an alternative theory that Mountbatten had put secret pressure on Radcliffe to ensure that the one last road and rail-link into Kashmir which stayed open throughout the winter – through Gurdaspur district – stayed in Indian territory. According to this theory, there must have been a Mountbatten–Congress plan to gain Kashmir from the start.

The future of Kashmir

Since 1947, there have been several full conflicts between India and Pakistan over Kashmir. A state of emergency has been in force from the 1990s to this day. Tens of thousands of Kashmiris have died in the continual fighting. There is little prospect of peace at the present time and the United Nations has identified Kashmir as the conflict most likely to cause the world's first nuclear exchange.

The end of Gandhi and Jinnah

Gandhi had been sidelined as the political momentum gathered towards independence. He was, however, still a respected figure. As communal violence erupted, and despite his age, he took himself to the centre of disturbances. In Bengal, he walked from village to village, insisting on calm before he moved on. He did not attempt the same in the Punjab; perhaps even he thought it beyond hope for a while.

He remained constant to his lifelong view that he should and could take personal responsibility for the violence and for promoting religious tolerance by example. He continued to include readings from the **Qur'an** at his prayer meetings and deliberately chose to be in a Muslim property on independence night. He let it be known that he was so distressed by the treatment of the Muslims that he was planning to spend what remained of his life in (East) Pakistan.

This was too much for some. At 5pm on the evening of 30 January 1948 he was walking to his evening prayer meeting among a crowd of supporters. Three shots were fired at close range into his chest. He died within minutes. It was later claimed that his last words were a prayer to the Hindu god Ram. More credible witnesses reported self-deprecation to the end: he said he hated being late for prayers.

His assassination was long-feared and leaders braced themselves for renewed communal attacks. However, it soon became clear that his killer, Nathuram Godse, was a Hindu fanatic, incensed by Gandhi's care for Muslims. Godse was a

Key date

Deaths of Gandhi and Jinnah: 1948

Key term

Qur'an
The Muslim holy book.

Exam tips

The cross-references are intended to take you straight to the material that will help you to answer the question.

Source 3 begins with the key issue of why independence was accompanied by partition. The question suggests that the prime reason for this was the threat of popular violence.

In support of the seriousness of the threat of popular violence, the following points can be developed from the sources:

- The Muslim League all-India council rejected constitutional methods and called for direct action in July 1946 (Source 1).
- Congress accepted partition because of fear of a revolutionary upsurge shown in the mass actions of 1946–7 (Source 3).
- Government was on the verge of collapse in 1946 (Source 2).

To counter the claim the following points can be developed from the sources:

- Partition was the result of political deadlock and disagreement between Congress and the League (Sources 2 and 3).
- Partition reflected the traditional Hindu–Muslim divisions (Source 3).
- Jinnah's statement (Source 1), in spite of the reference to 'pistol', is a call for mass civil disobedience – not for mass violence.

You should use your own knowledge from Chapter 5 to develop or counter these points, and to add new issues. You could consider:

- army and navy mutinies in 1946 (page 117)
- the electoral successes of both Congress and League in 1946 (page 118)
- the mistakes and misjudgements made by Indian and British politicians – in particular in relation to the cabinet mission (pages 118–22)
- the role of Jinnah (page 123 onward)
- the great Calcutta killings (pages 123–5)
- the role of Mountbatten (page 126 onward).

You will need to reach an overall conclusion. How far do you agree with the statement?

6 Surveying the Transfer of Power

How might one summarise the transition from imperial territory to independent nation in comparison to other similar forces and events?

1 | Character

A predominant feature of Indian history in the twentieth century would be its relative peacefulness, certainly in relation to the British ruling power. Of course, there were communal riots throughout the period and the terrible massacres of the partition but these were, comparatively speaking, localised and brief, however violent.

There was no revolutionary overthrow of power, despite the obvious numerical weakness of the British and the exhaustion of morale and resources after the Second World War. The British Raj lived with the collective fear of another Indian Mutiny but, in retrospect, the greatest danger was that the British would be exposed as powerless to stop escalating violence between Indians.

Similarly, there was no sustained support for terrorist or guerrilla tactics in fighting for freedom from the imperial power as happened in parts of the British Empire and in the empires of other European powers.

Indeed, the Indian nationalist movement is inextricably associated with the non-violent campaigns of Gandhi. Independence would have come without Gandhi but his leadership determined its character and legacy.

Moreover, the overwhelmingly trouble-free absorption of over 500 princely states into a huge modern democracy must be judged considerable progress.

Overall, those involved appear to have recognised historical forces at work, combined with practical problems and crises beyond the control of the British. The sheer scale of governing India perhaps engendered mutual caution, pragmatism and a certain respect.

Accordingly, rather than dramatic events, the history is characterised, literally, by personal political tactics played out across constitutional legislation.

2 | Gandhi and Churchill

In this regard, a remarkable feature of the history is the rather abrupt marginalisation of two of the great figures of the events and of the twentieth century: Gandhi and Churchill. In each case, the great leader became a problem and a liability to his cause and nation.

Gandhi sought integrity in his life's work. Spiritually, this involved a large amount of religious tolerance but ultimately his commitment was to Hindu power and responsibility. Politically and economically, his vision involved turning the clock back 1000 years. Knowing this was unrealistic, but unwilling to compromise personally, perhaps the most astute of Gandhi's many moves was to ensure that Nehru came to prominence in Congress. Nehru was modern, secular and socialist – the complete opposite of Gandhi – but he was the future for India and he was prepared to do the necessary political deals that Gandhi had less and less time for.

Churchill, like Gandhi, was driven by a conservative vision. In his case, it was imperial power and the moral obligation of white Europeans to govern other peoples for their own good. His refusal to contemplate independence, indeed his anger at the idea, exasperated political colleagues, not least President Roosevelt. Churchill was far-sighted in seeing the shape of the postwar world and thought that Britain's Empire could match, and would be needed to match, the two new superpowers of the USA and the Soviet Union. However, his vision, like Gandhi's, was out of step with the postwar desire of the British for a modern, socialist society. For a Britain impoverished by the Second World War, an affordable welfare state was more important than the pomp of empire.

3 | Jinnah and Pakistan

Jinnah, by contrast, appears to have achieved more success than he thought realistic. At the very start of the period, the last Mughal Emperor was deposed. For a long time, the Muslim League was not that well supported by Muslim voters. However, eventual election success, rejection of political cooperation by Congress and loyalty to the British during the war handed Jinnah the opportunity to make demands for Muslim recognition which, seemingly, led inexorably to the creation of Pakistan. Jinnah, secular and tolerant, found himself governor-general of a brand new Muslim nation-state.

The creation of Pakistan is the most debatable feature of the period. Descriptions of personal achievement beg the question by assuming that this was a desired, and desirable, goal. There is considerable evidence that all parties simply found themselves with dwindling time and will to pursue other solutions.

Jinnah and the Muslim League initially used vague demands for one or perhaps two separate Muslim states in the hope of a stronger position in a single India. Even at the end, support for the idea was strongest in areas well away from the territory likely to become Pakistan.

Nehru, Patel and Congress lost the political initiative in the drive towards independence created by the postwar British Labour government. Then they lost their patience and agreed with the Muslim demand, thinking that the new Pakistan would collapse, along with Muslim leadership, and be quickly reabsorbed into a Congress-dominated India.

4 | Partition

For the British, partition was more complicated than desired but certainly not unprecedented. They had done more or less the same in Ireland and had carved up the Ottoman Empire (including promising the territory of Palestine to both Arabs and Jews). Moreover, a loyal Muslim Pakistan brought strategic securities in the region to balance an India which was likely to be anti-British, pro-Soviet and pro-Communist China.

In the longer view, the partition massacres, which have been blamed on the hasty departure of the British, were also far from unique. For example, the break-up of Yugoslavia in the 1990s led to vicious ethnic conflict and, arguably, the conflict within Iraq is a struggle by religious and ethnic groups for regional control within an undesired state (created by the British).

5 | Looking to the Future

We should also note that, since independence, India has continued to suffer from internal religious violence, as well as wars with Pakistan and China, which also occupies Indian territory in the far north. However, its economy is now booming and the country looks set to be a global power in the twenty-first century.

Pakistan's history has been less happy. Jinnah's successor, Liaquat Ali Khan, was assassinated in 1951 and a military dictatorship held power until elections were finally held in 1969. In East Pakistan, a separatist party took every seat and when their leader, Sheikh Rahman, was arrested, a war of independence began in 1971. Indian troops intervened and the outcome was the fully recognised state of Bangladesh. Despite long-term support by the United States (and Britain), Pakistan remains a fragile, troubled state.

Viceroys of British India

1856–62	**Canning**	Charles, 1st Earl of Canning
1862–3	**Elgin**	Bruce, James, 8th Earl of Elgin
1863–9	**Lawrence**	Lawrence, Sir John
1869–72	**Mayo**	Bourke, Richard, 6th Earl of Mayo
1872–6	**Northbrook**	Baring, Thomas, 1st Earl of Northbrook
1876–80	**Lytton**	Edward, 1st Earl of Lytton
1880–4	**Ripon**	Robinson, George, 1st Marquess of Ripon
1884–8	**Dufferin**	Blackwood, Frederick, 1st Marquess of Dufferin & Ava
1888–94	**Lansdowne**	Petty-Fitzmaurice, Henry, 5th Marquess of Lansdowne
1894–8	**Elgin**	Bruce, Victor, 9th Earl of Elgin
1898–1905	**Curzon**	George, 1st Marquess Curzon of Keddleston
1905–10	**Minto**	Elliot, Gilbert, 4th Earl of Minto
1910–16	**Hardinge**	Charles, 1st Baron of Penshurst
1916–21	**Chelmsford**	Thesiger, Frederic, 1st Viscount Chelmsford
1921–6	**Reading**	Isaacs, Rufus, 1st Marquess of Reading
1926–31	**Irwin**	Wood, Edward, Lord Irwin & 1st Earl of Halifax
1931–6	**Willingdon**	Freeman-Thomas, Freeman, 1st Marquess of Willingdon
1936–43	**Linlithgow**	Hope, Victor, 2nd Marquess of Linlithgow
1943–7	**Wavell**	Wavell, Archibald, 1st Viscount & Earl Wavell
1947	**Mountbatten**	Mountbatten, Louis, 1st Viscount & Earl Mountbatten

Glossary

Accession   The process of peacefully merging into a larger country.

Ahimsa   Literal meaning is non-violence.

Annexation   Forced but peaceful conquest of territory.

Ashram   Small religious, often farming, community.

Babu   Bengali term for clerk.

Bolshevik   A member of the majority, thus the political group that emerged as leader of the revolution.

Cartographical   Relating to maps.

Caste   A rigid public social division. Derived from a Portuguese word.

Censure   A formal political reprimand.

Communal   Relating to a religious community across the whole population.

Communism   The political philosophy of a classless society with workers in power; ideology of the Soviet Union.

Congress   A meeting.

Constituent assembly   A parliament with the sole task of designing a constitution.

Contiguous   A formal term for touching or adjoining.

Cottage industry   Pre-factory organisation of home weaving or workshops, for example.

Demobilised   Released from the armed forces.

Demographic   Relating to population.

Dhoti   Loin cloth.

District   A formal subdivision of a province.

Divide and rule   Imperialist strategy, from Romans onward, of provoking enmities to prevent subject groups uniting in opposition.

Dominion status   A category of self-government within the British Empire denoting a full nation.

Durbar   Imperial celebration.

Dyarchy   Obscure term from classical Greek meaning two-part power.

Excise   A tax on goods made inside the country.

Federal   Government with considerable regional powers.

For the duration   Became a common phrase to describe the unknown length of the war.

Franchise   The conditions making people eligible to vote.

Ghadr   Translates as mutiny.

The Great Game   The spying and skirmishing that accompanied the continuing Russo-British rivalry and competition.

Gurdwara   Sikh temple.

Hansard   Published transcripts of parliamentary debates.

Harijans   Translates as sons of god.

Hartal   Strike action, refusal to work.

Hindustan   Literally the land beyond the Indus (coming from the west) – an Arab or Mughal perspective.

Home affairs   Government department for law, order and justice.

Hostage theory   Vulnerable minorities in each country would ensure mutual protection.

Indigenous   People native to a place (but not primitive).

Indigo   Purple dye from the leaves of a plant.

Insurgency   A prolonged uprising.

Interned   Imprisoned without trial.

Jatha   A squad.

Khadi   Home-spun cloth or clothing.

Khalifah   Deputy of the founder of Islam, sometimes caliph.

Khilafat   Campaign to protect the last link with the medieval caliphs or deputies of the prophet Muhammad.

Lathi   A steel-tipped cane.

Mahasabha   Literally meaning great association.

Mandated   Instructed by a political organisation.

Martial law   Army imposes its own rules, suspends civil courts and justice.

Mesopotamia   The Middle East, especially now Iraq, from the Greek for between rivers (the Tigris and Euphrates in Iraq).

Minute   An official document.

Official opposition   The largest minority group in a parliament.

Orders-in-council   Legislation approved by a viceroy without full parliamentary scrutiny.

Ottoman Empire   Islamic Empire of the Middle East and modern Turkey.

Pacifism   Refusal to fight in wartime.

Pact   An agreement between political allies.

Panchayat   Assembly (originally of five village elders).

Pandemic   Global epidemic.

Paramount power   A diplomatic term for the most powerful force, often an occupying army.

Parsi   Ancient Iranian religion.

Partition   The formal division of a state or province.

Peripatetic   Moving round from one workplace to another.

Plebiscite   A vote of the whole population on constitutional issues.

Plenipotentiary powers   The capacity to make decisions without approval from government.

Polytheistic   A religion with many gods and goddesses.

Proto-nationalist   A first example or experiment, before adoption of the aims of nationalism.

Punjab   Meaning five rivers.

Purna swaraj   Total independence.

Qur'an   The Muslim holy book.

R.I.   *Rex Imperator*, Latin for King-Emperor.

Realpolitik   A term for political leverage, borrowed from the German language.

Renaissance A rebirth or flowering of culture.

Resolution A formal decision at a meeting, often voted on.

Round table conference A meeting of comprehensive inclusion with all opinions equally considered.

Rupee The currency of India.

Sabha An association.

Sacred cow In Hinduism actual cows are sacred; the term is widely used to indicate a protected idea.

Sanskrit An ancient Indian language.

Satyagraha Literal meaning is truth-force or soul-force.

Scapegoat A person chosen to carry the blame for others.

Scheduled castes Political term for the lowest caste, commonly known as untouchables or dalits.

Secede Peacefully break away from a state.

Secular Public, non-religious affairs.

Seditious Encouraging overthrow of a government.

Sepoy An Indian soldier.

Surety A deposit lost in the event of breaking the law.

Swadesh A campaign not to buy something – known as a boycott in English.

Swaraj Literally self-rule, thus meaning independence.

Ulster Province in Ireland allowed to remain British.

Viceroy The deputy for a monarch.

White Man's Burden The perceived duty to govern so-called inferior races and countries.

White paper A firm set of proposals for legislation.

Index